COMPASS POINTS: A PRACTICAL GUIDE TO POETRY FORMS

If I was to choose any poet to enhance the Compass Points series it would be Alison Chisholm. She has a no-nonsense approach to teaching poetry that can be fully understood by non-poets (like myself) and is a highly respected poet in her own right. She wrote the poetry correspondence course for The Writers' Bureau, which has been going for many years. This is a 'must have' book.
Suzanne Ruthven

Most 'would-be' poets are so busy exploring the 'what' of their writing – the ideas, subject, meaning, content – that they overlook the 'how' – the shape, techniques, means, form. Alison Chisholm's new book *Compass Points: A Practical Guide to Poetry Forms* is indispensable. In 8 clear chapters she explores the nature of different metrical and rhythmic approaches, and explains in an authoritative and accessible manner the wide variety of available poetic forms, from couplet to free verse. Her exploration is supported by a wide range of appropriate poetic examples, and each chapter is capped by a series of sensibly-challenging exercises. The result? An indispensable book – and not only for the new-comer. Whatever level of your craft, I urge you to buy it; read it; and use it. You'll be surprised at what you'll achieve for your writing and your self.
Roger Elkin

Alison Chisholm's new handbook should be essential reading for all aspiring poets, and many experienced writers will also find her guidance and explanations to be invaluable, as it serves as a refresher c   ıs.
Stephen W

A well published and technically adept poet herself, Alison Chisholm defines in a lucid manner the many forms and variants that can be used in poetry. She explains a number of factors giving excellent examples and exercises. With her usual expertise Alison guides us through combinations of content and technique. She is precise in this, but her intriguing observations and suggestions ensure that the enjoyment of writing a poem is not lost in the technical detail being discussed. This is a book to be read, dipped into and retained permanently on your bookshelf.

Doris Corti

Compass Points: A Practical Guide to Poetry Forms

How to Find the Perfect Form for Your Poem

Compass Points:
A Practical Guide
to Poetry Forms

How to Find the Perfect Form for Your Poem

Alison Chisholm

**COMPASS
BOOKS**

Winchester, UK
Washington, USA

First published by Compass Books, 2014
Compass Books is an imprint of John Hunt Publishing Ltd., Laurel House, Station Approach, Alresford, Hants, SO24 9JH, UK
office1@jhpbooks.net
www.johnhuntpublishing.com
www.compass-books.net

For distributor details and how to order please visit the 'Ordering' section on our website.

Text copyright: Alison Chisholm 2013

ISBN: 978 1 78279 032 7

A CIP catalogue record for this book is available from the British Library.

Design: Lee Nash

Printed and bound by CPI Group (UK) Ltd, Croydon, CR0 4YY

We operate a distinctive and ethical publishing philosophy in all areas of our business, from our global network of authors to production and worldwide distribution.

CONTENTS

BOOKS BY THE SAME AUTHOR

The Craft of Writing Poetry
A Practical Poetry Course
How to Write 5-Minute Features
How to Write About Yourself (with Brenda Courtie)
Writing Competitions: The Way to Win (with Iain Pattison)
The Handy Little Book of Tips for Poets
Crafting Poetry
The Poet's Workbook

POETRY COLLECTIONS

Alone No More (with Robin Gregory)
Flying Free
Single Return
The Need for Unicorns
Paper Birds
Light Angles
Daring the Slipstream
Mapping the Maze
Hold Tight
Iced
Star and Snowflake

Preface

Whatever your experience of poetry, an understanding of set form will enhance your enjoyment of it. This book examines over fifty forms and variants, with information on strict metres, fixed and variable lengths, full and slant rhyme, syllabic and spatial poetry, free verse and blank verse, as well as assistance with devising your own variations and crafting new forms.

It is crammed with tips, examples to demonstrate the different techniques, and exercises to enrich your writing skills. Dip, read, absorb and enjoy.

Happy writing.

Chapter 1

The Concept of Form

Being a poet is an amazing calling. Whether you feel it's your life's work or just a pleasant pastime, it places you in an elite group of people whose ranks include Homer, Sappho, Chaucer, Shakespeare, Wordsworth, Eliot, Plath and Motion. It shows you the world in a new and exciting way, and allows you to communicate that excitement with people you will never meet, but whose lives are affected by what you have said.

Your poems will be crammed with ideas and insights, emotion and reaction, observation and perception. The vehicle for conveying these depends on imagery, use of language, rhythm, metaphor and other elements; but before these can work, it needs a form.

As soon as you start to write your poem down, a form, its physical structure, begins to emerge. As it takes shape, it may evolve a pattern of its own, or it may be worked into one of the set forms that have been developed, practised and perfected over generations. Poets of the past have left a legacy of templates that work. If they didn't we would not still be using them.

Some forms lend themselves to particular themes and subjects. Sonnets, for example, are often used for love poetry. Others convey a mood or atmosphere, like the haunting villanelle whose repetitions give it an enclosed, almost claustrophobic feel.

The skill of marrying content and form, acquired as much by practice as study, gives your poetry an edge - the advantage of working well in patterns poets inherit and readers recognise. Understanding the dynamics of different forms adds to the enjoyment of the poetry you read, and enriches the quality of the poetry you write.

Playing with forms can be exhilarating and exasperating,

often at the same time. It's easy to be whipped along by the excitement of the moment, and glory in the joy of fitting all the words into a sestina, getting the repetition right in a pantoum, or finding the perfect Zen moment for a haiku. These are, indeed, moments to be enjoyed and relished; but never at the expense of the quality of the poem. It's always a case of poetry first, nuts and bolts after.

For the writer, there is something reassuring about using a set form. It provides you with a framework into which you can fit the information you want to communicate in the poem. It tells you where lines and/or stanzas begin and end, and how the rhymes fit. Apply it correctly, and it gives your poem shape, authority and confidence.

For the reader, a set form gives the assurance that this poem has direction, a planned route through its content, which indicates that safe hands are providing guidance to help you understand what it has to say.

The form indicates the number and length of lines, their metre, and the placing of rhymes and repetitions. This involves some ancient Greek terms and a touch of alphabet juggling, but it's worth persevering with these. Let's start with the lines.

Some forms have fixed numbers of lines, while others may be broken down into a sequence of verses or stanzas. Limericks have five lines, for example, triolets eight, and rubais a multiple of four, as they can be written in any number of four-line stanzas. The line length is the second half of the metrical description, but we'll look at it first. (We're poets, we're allowed to be contrary.) It may be:

Monometerone measure - or foot - in the line

Dimeter	two feet
Trimeter	three feet
Tetrameter	four feet
Pentameter	five feet

Hexameter	six feet
Heptameter	seven feet
Octameter	eight feet

The first half of the phrase is the definition of each foot, depending on the emphasis natural pronunciation gives to a word, part of a word, or a phrase. It's the metre, this pattern of stressed and unstressed syllables, that gives the lines a beat, and the major ones are these:

Pyrrhic	two unstressed syllables	of a
Spondee	two stressed	strange times
Iamb/iambus	one unstressed, one stressed	behind
Trochee	one stressed, one unstressed	Friday
Anapaest	two unstressed, one stressed	in the house
Dactyl	one stressed, two unstressed	heartily
Anti-bacchic	one unstressed, two stressed	a long night
Bacchic	two stressed, one unstressed	deep breathing
Amphibrach	one unstressed, one stressed, one unstressed	behaviour
Amphimacer	one stressed, one unstressed, one stressed	candle wax
Tribrach	three unstressed	if it is
Molossus	three stressed	four train guards

The metrical foot most often used in the English language is the one that fits most naturally into the way words are pronounced. This is the iambic foot, often in the pentameter version. So a single line of iambic pentameter consists of five feet, each of two syllables - the first unstressed, and the second stressed. Try saying this line aloud, and the pronunciation should fall neatly into the pattern:

He rode the horse across the furrowed field.

To avoid any possible misreading, the line can be marked with x to indicate an unstressed syllable, and / for a stressed one:

```
x  /   x  /   x /   x  / x     /
```
He rode the horse across the furrowed field.

Iambic tetrameter, with lines a foot (two syllables) shorter, is second in popularity:

```
x  /   x  /   x /   x  /
```
He rode the horse across the field.

Following close behind is iambic hexameter, with its six feet, also known as the alexandrine. Some forms end a stanza of iambic pentameter with an alexandrine or two.

```
x  /   x /   x  /   x /   x  /   x     /
```
He rode a chestnut horse across the furrowed field

Once a pattern such as iambic pentameter is established, it's important to keep to it throughout the poem, unless you are changing it for a sound artistic reason; but it would become very dull if it were pounded out for hundreds of lines without a single variant. It's a good idea to practise unvaried metre until it becomes second nature, and then to look at the tiny syncopations that work within it.

The first of these frequently used variants is initial trochaic substitution, where you replace the first iambus with a trochee, so that the line begins with a stressed syllable followed by an unstressed, and then reverts to the usual form, eg:

```
/  x  x /   x /   x  /   x     /
```
Riding a horse across the furrowed field

This gives a pleasing effect, but it's important to remember to change back to the familiar pattern in the second foot.

The other change that often occurs is the addition of an unstressed syllable at the end of the line, or feminine ending:

x / x /   x /   x / x / x
He rode a horse across the grassy meadow.

This gives a lingering note to the end of the line, and again makes an attractive change. (The less usual additional stressed syllable is a masculine ending.)

Iambic pentameters produced without rhyme are known as blank verse, a good device for conveying a narrative poem. It's the form we find in the main body of Shakespeare's plays, (although he does include occasional fully rhymed extracts and also some prose.) Wordsworth's autobiographical work, *The Prelude*, is also written in blank verse, and this form is dealt with in more detail in Chapter 5.

It's always useful to read developing poems aloud, as it gives a new angle on them. When you are assessing your use of metre and line length it's especially important, as any hiccups are discovered by the ear as readily as the eye.

The alphabet juggling comes with the addition of rhyme to the lines, as letters are used to indicate where rhymes fall. Each time a new full (exact) rhyme sound is introduced, it's assigned the next letter of the alphabet. Appearing in lower case means that it will rhyme, whereas upper case means that it will be repeated, often alongside other repeated words or maybe the whole line. If a number of lines rhyming together are repeated, an alphanumeric system is used: A1 A2 A3, B1 B2 etc. If a sound is not going to rhyme with anything, the letter x appears.

The shades of night   A

were lifting, light	a
expelling shadows,	x
drawing day.	b
The shades of night	A
were put to flight.	a
He shuddered, wept	x
and tried to pray.	b
He never knew	c
that she wept too.	c

Further rhyme sounds would be designated d, e, f, and so on with R standing for a refrain, (repeated word/s usually appearing between stanzas,) and a forward slash denoting slant rhyme with its sound similarity, rather than full rhyme.

If you do not already have one, a rhyming dictionary, on paper or electronic, is a vital piece of equipment for anyone wanting to write in set forms. Some people worry that this is a form of cheating. That is most definitely not the case. The rhyming dictionary does not give you the answers; it simply sets out the possibilities so that you can make your choice. It bypasses some of the poetry spadework, allowing you more time and creative energy to concentrate on the poem itself, rather than on the mechanics of construction. Think of it as a tool that helps with the job, and it will become your best friend.

By the end of the twentieth century, over 250 forms were in regular use. The communications explosion of the internet has seen that number increase wildly. New forms are being proposed all the time, some more successful than others. This means that there's nearly always a form available for the poem you want to write. Many of the forms discussed in this book are accompanied by suggestions for the type of content that could work well in them.

The forms are explained according to any combination of the elements of number of lines or stanzas, line length, metre, rhyme, word or syllable count, and shape. If you don't enjoy the idea of working from statistics, you can use the examples as a template, fitting your own subject matter into the same pattern. Do still look at the statistical bit, though, as there are often alternatives offered which are not shown as separate examples.

This same practice can, of course, be continued in the wider world of poetry, in both set form patterns and free verse. The devices for conveying a poem you read may strike you as a brilliant idea for communicating something you're wishing to say, but can't work out how to begin. A device as simple as starting the poem with a phrase like *I hate it when...* can be enough for you to emulate in order to kickstart your own material. By all means make good use of any such source, and you may trigger a brilliant poem from it.

Always remember, though, that your finished poem must be yours. You don't want it to appear like a pale imitation of someone else's. Make sure your subject matter is vastly different from theirs; and when you have completed the poem fitting the template that inspired you, make enough adjustments to your writing for it to be impossible to identify its source. Then you will have the satisfaction of knowing you have written an original piece, and will not be kept awake by anxieties about a suit for plagiarism.

Usually the selection of form is instinctive, but sometimes it helps to have a hint of guidance. However experienced a poet is, there's always a chance that things could go wrong, resulting in a thought-provoking poem to be delivered at a funeral produced in jaunty rhyming couplets, or a light, frothy subject in ponderous iambic hexameters.

If you have the slightest uncertainty about the best form for a subject, it's useful to try it out in a range of different forms. Sometimes you can surprise yourself by experimenting with a form on the off-chance it might work... only to find it's the perfect vehicle for your idea. And if you decide that half a dozen experiments didn't work, you can remind yourself that it wasn't a waste of time. The experience of trying out the forms adds to both your writing skills and your understanding of the relationship between subject and form.

The following exercises are designed to help you get the most practical help from the information in this book. They are, where possible, open enough to allow you to return to them repeatedly and produce new work. Some are designed to put into practice theoretical points we have considered. Others will lead to complete poems. And in case you have the slightest doubt about these, remember that it doesn't matter whether a poem started as an inspirational bolt from the blue or from the slog of an exercise; it's where you take the germ of an idea - and what you do with it - that counts.

Exercises

1. Following the example of the line about the man riding a horse, create a single line of iambic pentameter, then adapt it to iambic tetrameter, as an alexandrine, then with initial trochaic substitution, and finally with a feminine ending. Which version pleases you most? How have the meaning and grammar altered with the adjustments?

2. Select any nursery rhyme and see whether you can identify the key metre it uses. The reason for using nursery rhymes is that they tend to have a regular beat, and you can recite them without looking at the page. The reason for 'key' metre is because there are often variations part way through the verse. If the idea of identifying the feet is too tedious, simply say them aloud to yourself and listen to the metrical patterns.

3. Take any rhymed poem you have not read before, and mark the rhymes alphabetically as indicated in the *Shades*

of night verse. Leave it for a day or two. Return to the poem and, without re-reading it, make a note of the combination of letters. Now write your own poem on a different theme, reproducing the rhyme scheme. When you have finished, compare your version with the original to check that rhymes have been placed in the same positions.

4. Read aloud some nineteenth or late eighteenth century poetry. Even if the poem sounds less magical, let your voice over-stress the weightier syllables of the line, and under-stress the lighter ones. Can you spot irregularities in the poem? Are they subtle or glaring? Can you identify what the poem was doing there?

5. Pick any line length except pentameter from the list, and write a few lines to the length in iambic feet on any subject. Now write lines to the same length in trochaic feet.

6. Write a poem - rhymed or unrhymed - in amphibrachic dimeter beginning with the word 'Remember.' If you wish, make some of the lines, placed at regular intervals, a syllable shorter (catalectic lines,) as demonstrated:

Remember the teacher
who gave inspiration
to prompt you to follow   (each line two amphibrachs)
the path to your dreams.   (catalectic)

Incidentally, a line may have an unstressed syllable missing at its start. This is referred to as acephalous.

Chapter 2

Short and Simple

Rhyming Couplets

The simplest form of poetry is the rhyming couplet, where two consecutive lines rhyme together. This gives the rhyme pattern: a a and can be continued to form: a a b b c c d d etc. It's easy to write and easy to remember. In fact, many of the first verses we learned by heart as children use rhyming couplets, such as:

Humpty Dumpty sat on a wall,   a

Humpty Dumpty had a great fall ...   a

followed by another couplet with a different rhyming sound:

All the King's horses and all the King's men   b
Couldn't put Humpty together again.   b

This nursery rhyme introduces two points of interest to the poet. First, in addition to the rhymes it is full of repetition, with the name and the references to *All the King's*. This type of deliberate repetition is used to reinforce the sense of poetry - and is distinct from accidental repeats, where unintentional over-use of a word can become tedious.

Also, there is an example in the second rhyme of a sound which may lose its impact through pronunciation. Although the *men/again* rhyme works perfectly in standard English, some regional variations result in the use of the *-ay* sound rather than the *-e*, to give *ag-ay-n* instead of *ag-e-n*. You can spot this phenomenon, too, when poets write within the pronunciation of their regional accent. Wordsworth, for example, rhymes *matter* with *water*, and of course he would have used the short -*a* sound in both words.

A few mnemonics use rhyming couplets, eg.

In fourteen hundred and ninety-two
Columbus sailed the ocean blue

and, still in the realms of history:

In AD sixteen sixty-six
London burned like rotten sticks.

Neither of these would be seen as great poetry; but if poems are intended to be memorable, they more than serve their purpose, fixing the dates in schoolchildren's heads.

A poem in rhyming couplets can be of any length, from the basic two-liner to Alexander Pope's interminable *The Rape of the Lock*. Nowadays the form is found most frequently in humorous poetry, partly, perhaps, because there's an irresistible urge to intone the infamous *Boom Boom* at the end of a rhymed couplet poem. It's difficult to imagine a contemporary poem on a serious or solemn theme in these couplets.

If you are going to use the form effectively, it's important in most cases to observe the same line length and metrical pattern throughout. This is especially important if you are writing comic verse, which requires absolute precision of metrical accuracy if it is not to lose its dynamic effect.

The exception is the poem that creates its own harmony of approach by deliberately avoiding regular line lengths and metre. There is scope for producing a narrative poem that subverts the idea of regularity completely. Try saying these few lines aloud:

In a gap in the traffic on the M62   a
is a gambler. Well, what is a mouse expected to do   a

when some murine obligation   b
calls her to leave the safety of shadows, yield to temptation   b
and cross?   c
Never considering the risk of loss   c
of life, she picks herself up on her delicate toes,   d
sniffs, and hitches her tail, and goes ...   d

The rhyme allows a sense of poetry, while the absence of strict metre and variance of line length provide an anecdotal touch. Here, too, the form needs to be applied. A sudden lapse into matching line lengths and metre would be as damaging to this piece as a movement away from these elements in a more formal pattern.

A problem inherent in rhyming couplets is that the rhymes appear in close proximity to each other. It is important, therefore, to be aware of the two biggest rhyme crimes in the language, and avoid them. These are the inclusion of a tired, illogical or otherwise unsuitable word simply to create a chiming sound; and adjustment of the syntax, wrenching the word order to place a rhyme at the line's end. You could have a couplet reading:

We watched the passing of the light
as sunset drifted into night.

Using unsuitable vocabulary could produce the illogical:

We watched the passing of the light
as sunset drifted like a kite.

Twisting the words might make the tortuous:

We watched the passing of the light.
The sun set, and then fell the night.

Although the same advice applies to every form, it is particularly noticeable in rhyming couplets.

One final point to consider whenever rhyme occurs is the importance of avoiding using the same chiming sound twice in rapid succession, or a very similar sound. It would be fine to use this sequence of rhymes in a couplet or quatrain poem: *day/play   mat/cat cheer/year   sun/done   nose/toes   flight/night*, but a mistake to rely on these: *day/play   rain/chain   they/sway   arrange/strange   late/state.*

Qasida

Proving there's an exception to every rule, this Arabic form consists of any number of couplets, often fifty or more, up to a maximum of a hundred, taking the same rhyming sound. All the lines are of the same length and metre. An elegant structure in its original languages, with a set route to follow, it is difficult to sustain in English. It's an excellent exercise for practising rhyming skills.

It is usually written in three sections, often as a panegyric, but variants include satire, seasons and the natural world.

APRIL

As warmer days announce it's spring,	a
bulbs stir and grow, birds start to sing,	a
and first sun cheers up everything.	a
Now dragonflies are on the wing	a
and apple trees are offering	a
their buds and blossom, promising	a
their autumn fruits. A fairy ring	a
bedecks the grass, acknowledging	a
the season's started with a zing.	a

This example illustrates how tedious the rhyming can become. The best thing to be said about it is that it falls short of the two hundred lines by a good long way.

Limericks

A neat form that makes use of a rhyming couplet sandwiched inside three lines that rhyme together is the limerick. This rhymes: a a b b a   and nearly always carries a humorous message, often a risqué one.

The three lines are longer than the couplet, and the beat of the poem needs to be regular. The basic metre provides one iambus and two anapaests in each of the longer lines, and one iambus and one anapaest in the shorter lines, giving the familiar pattern of:

A foolish young fellow from Bow	a
decided to sleep in the snow.	a
He woke up quite numb	b
from shoulder to bum	b
and frozen from topknot to toe.	a

This standard metrical format can be varied slightly, as long as the rhythm still flows. The next example shows an additional unstressed syllable placed at the end of each of the long lines, and another at the start of the last three lines.

A poet whose writings were torrid	a
wrote overblown verse, wild and florid.	a
His sestinas lacked style,	b
terza rimas were vile,	b
and his sonnets were perfectly horrid.	a

There is still a regular beat, and again the piece works as a limerick.

It's easier to judge the effectiveness of a limerick when you say the poem aloud. If you have to elide sounds together or hear hiccups in the rhythm, the verse needs more attention.

Limericks, like haikus, don't usually have titles. They often begin with a character identified by a name, occupation or place, although this is not a requirement of the form.

In the past, convention provided a near-repeat of the first line at the end, but this meant that the joke fell flat, and has fallen out of favour. Consider how the two limericks above would be weakened if the final lines read: *that foolish young fellow from Bow* and *that poet whose writings were torrid* respectively.

Tercets

The tercet, or triplet, has three lines. It may be a three line poem, rhymed or unrhymed, or more usually, the stanza pattern for a poem.

Enclosed Tercet

This version can be written in any metre, but rhymes: a x a. It is close to the brevity of a couplet, but has the advantage of the unrhymed line between the two rhyming ones. This extra distance between the rhymes is invaluable, as there is more leeway for the language to move, and so you are less likely to fall into any of the couplet traps.

This poem uses trochaic trimeter, but each line is catalectic.

PASSING

Scarlet poppies line the lane. a

Hearses pass each day, each day, x
meeting military planes. /a

Khaki clothes exchanged for shrouds b
leave wives weeping, mums bereft, x
sun displaced by thunderclouds. b

Futures wrecked and plans destroyed, c
toppled - clichéd house of cards; x
life has turned into a void. c

Blood red poppies wither, die   d
leaving just a hard, cold shell;   x
desiccated, bleak goodbye.   d

Sicilian Tercet

This uses the same rhyme pattern as the enclosed tercet, but takes iambic pentameter. Again like the enclosed version, it is a good vehicle for a lyric or, as in this case, a short narrative.

MIDNIGHT

The handle turned. She gave a start of fear.   a

It must have been a dream – and yet she thought…   x
Her heartbeat quickened. No one should be here.   a

She held her breath, lay shivering in bed,   b
and heard a muffled footstep at her door.   x
A knot of terror twisted in her head.   b

She had to tell herself - and to believe -   c
of course she was alone, and she was safe,   x
for what would giving in to fear achieve?   c

There could be no intruder, and she knew   d
that ghosts did not exist. Her mind, fatigued,   x
was playing tricks; no need to think this through.   d

Determinedly affecting unconcern   e
she settled down to sleep and closed her eyes;   x
and so she didn't see the handle turn…   e

Triversen

The triversen stanza is a native American form, which was developed by William Carlos Williams and other poets. Its name is a composite of *triple verse sentence*, and it consists of six tercets, each of which is made up of a single sentence, or sometimes a clause. So grammar and sentence structuring are an essential element of its construction.

The sentence is divided into three phrases, to produce the three lines of the tercet. Full rhyme is not used, nor is strict metre, but there is one important point about the stressed syllables of the line. Lines may be of varied lengths, but there should be two, three or four stressed syllables in each.

LEARNING THE ROAD

This road has no end;
   it started with a decision to walk,
      ambles on through unremitting green.

You may want to escape your mind's muddle,
   but mile on monotonous mile
      the same horizon lours.

Still air smells stale;
   even your passing fails to stir it
      through the mustiness of leaves.

Time is trapped,
   seconds cobwebbed
      where twig and branch turn bone.

You count the rickety fence posts,
   count your own breaths
      until there are no numbers left.

At last you dare to look back,
    trace the road's twists into infinity;
        wonder where to go next.

Quatrains

A quatrain is any stanza of four lines, rhymed or unrhymed, and again it may be a complete poem in itself or the stanza pattern for a poem.

Ballad Stanza

As its name suggests, this is an ideal form for communicating a narrative poem, telling the story through any number of stanzas. The first and third lines are written in iambic tetrameter and the second and fourth in iambic trimeter. The shorter lines rhyme, to give: x a x a x b x b x c x c and so on, demonstrated in these stanzas from the re-telling of a fairy tale.

I'd never seen their grey stone house,   x

    but something made me go   a
along the darkest forest tracks   x
    where poisonous toadstools grow.   a

Who's there? a thin, high voice called out,   x
    and *won't you come indoors?*   b
I didn't want to, but my feet   x
    were dragged by some strange force.   b

The room was small and cold and cramped,   x
    no fire burned, no lamp gleamed;   c
the women smiled, and handed me   x
    a cup that gently steamed.   c

Do take some cordial with us,	x
one said, *and sit a while.*	d
I had no choice. My own hand made	x
me drink. The taste was vile.	d
The other one began to say	x
how visitors were few,	e
but when they came they never left…	x
and I would stay there too.	e

Ballad stanzas also work well as jokes in verse, or as descriptive poems.

A variant is hymnal stanza, which sees rhyme in the shorter first and third lines as well as in the second and fourth, making a pattern of: a b a b   c d c d   e f e f   etc.

Rubai

This is an attractive quatrain form, and again there is no fixed length so the poem can be made up of any number of rubais, or rubaiyat. The form is Arabic, and perhaps the best known example is found in the work attributed to Omar Khayyam, the eleventh century Persian poet and mathematician, and most famously translated by Edward FitzGerald.

Rubais are slightly more difficult to construct than ballad stanzas, as three words are required for each rhyme instead of two. The first, second and fourth lines rhyme, while the third produces a different sound, forming: a a x a. The metre is iambic pentameter or tetrameter.

Although the form has been identified with philosophical themes, it works with a range of subjects. Here's a frivolous example:

DINNER DATE

The restaurant is noise and bustle, hot	a
with jazz and steak, a pulsing melting pot	a
of waiters, barmen, Dads with hyper kids.	x
I have no wish to dine with this coarse lot.	a
I long for romance - crystal, candles; eyes	b
exchanging loving glances. Compromise	b
is not an option. If he thinks I'd like	x
to eat here, he is in for a surprise.	b
Tonight is more disaster than a date.	c
It's time to cut my losses, leave. But wait -	c
a gorgeous waiter smiles at me and winks.	x
I'll smile back, and I'll leave the rest to fate.	c

A delightful tweak to this form is to craft interlocking rubais. Instead of placing an unrhymed line in each stanza, the third line chimes with the main rhyme in the following stanza. The final stanza's third line brings the poem full circle by chiming with the main rhyme from the opening stanza. In a four-stanza version, then, the rhyme scheme would be: a a b a b b c b c c d c d d a d.

Adapting the example given above to an interlocking format would read something like this:

DINNER DATE

The restaurant is noise and bustle, hot	a
with jazz and steak, a pulsing melting pot	a
of waiters, barmen, kids demanding fries.	b
I have no wish to dine with this coarse lot.	a

I long for romance - crystal, candles; eyes	b
exchanging loving glances. Compromise	b
is not an option. If he thinks I'd rate	c
a meal here, he is in for a surprise.	b

Tonight is more disaster than a date.	c
It's time to cut my losses, leave. But wait -	c
a gorgeous waiter smiles and winks a lot.	a
I'll smile back, and I'll leave the rest to fate.	c

Read both versions aloud, and you will appreciate the different techniques the poet requires and the effect created by the chain (interlocking) rhyme.

Italian Envelope Stanza

An elegant quatrain in iambic pentameters is the Italian envelope. In this, a rhyming couplet is tucked inside another two rhyming lines: a b b a. Any number of these stanzas can be used to make up a poem. The form lends itself to a wide range of subject matter, and is often applied to material designed to make the reader think, as this example shows.

FREE GIFT

No matter who we are or how we feel,	a
what strange, capricious thoughts may fill our head,	b
our preference to lead or to be led,	b
our limitations, fanciful or real;	a

no matter how we look, our gender, size,	c
skin's colour, or the way we stand or move,	d
whatever things we hate, and whom we love;	/d
what songs we sing, what treasures we may prize;	c

22

no matter if we choose to travel far	e
or stay near home, the way we spend our days,	f
what terrors scare and what delights amaze,	f
our work or leisure, how content we are;	e

whatever power we think is in control,	g
what deity, what spirit of the earth	h
or air, resolved to nurture us from birth;	h
saw fit to grant the gift of life to all.	/g

Incidentally, there are two points about this poem which should be noted. First, it comprises just a single sentence. This is an unusual and controversial format. The grammar is intact, but the sentence length seems preposterous. Only the careful moulding in the poem's pattern allows it to make sense. This is largely due to the clear and logical format of the envelope stanza.

Two of the stanzas feature inexact rhymes: *move/love* (stanza 2) *control/all* (stanza 4.) These have been marked with a forward slash as slant rhymes on the text. Deviation from the precise rhyme can be good for adding a hint of variety to a regular pattern, as long as the slant rhyming sounds are very similar. There are no rules as to what constitutes 'very similar.' Try out each case with the eye and the ear, and instinct will inform you if it works.

Redondilla

This Spanish quatrain varies from other forms we've considered as it is written in iambic tetrameters throughout. It may rhyme: a b b a, a b a b, or a a b b. When it is used as a stanza form, it usually takes the same rhyme pattern in each stanza. The first rhyme scheme mentioned, a b b a, is also known as the In Memoriam stanza, taking its name from Tennyson's poem in memory of his friend Arthur Henry Hallam. These lines show how the different rhyme patterns compare.

When snow lies thick on field and tree,	a
a frosted tingle in the air	b
spins icy cobwebs in your hair	b
in winter's mystic tracery.	a

Or:

When snow lies thick on field and tree,	a
a frosted tingle in the air	b
in winter's mystic tracery	a
spins icy cobwebs in your hair.	b

Or:

When snow lies thick on field and tree	a
in winter's mystic tracery,	a
a frosted tingle in the air	b
spins icy cobwebs in your hair.	b

Clerihew

A fun form, and a complete poem rather than a stanza pattern, this is named after Edmund Clerihew Bentley, the humourist who invented it at the beginning of the twentieth century. It's a brief quatrain in two rhyming couplets: a a b b. A requirement is that there should be some disparity in the line lengths. The poem is biographical and often humorous, and the first line of the poem consists of the name of its subject. It does not usually have a title.

John William Anglin	a
left the Feds dangling	a
when he escaped. And you can bet	b
he's missing yet.	b

Exercises

7. Write a series of rhyming couplets creating a humorous story that tells a joke. Use strict metre and set line lengths, or allow yourself the same latitude as the example about the mouse exhibits. If you feel energised, try both.

8. Write a limerick about someone who lives in Kent. Make sure that you adhere to the rhythm. Read it to somebody else - or better still, get them to read it to you - to check that the pattern works. Try another limerick, this time one that doesn't feature a place name at the end of the first line.

9. Tell a familiar tale in ballad stanza, and give it a twist; eg. tell the sequel to Goldilocks, where three bears break in and mess up her cottage, or narrate the unpleasantness of King Canute and the waves, told in the voice of the laundry maid who is not impressed by all the seawater she has to clean out of his clothes.

10. Write four rubais about some aspect of the natural world – a description of a hedgerow, the effect of rain on the garden, etc. Now rework them as interlocking rubais. Which do you prefer, and why?

11. Try a few Italian envelope or In Memoriam stanzas (iambic pentameter or tetrameter) on the theme of autumn, using description but avoiding the clichés of russet leaves and swirling smoke.

12. Construct a clerihew about someone you know personally and dislike, or about someone you can't stand who is in the public eye. Politicians make wonderful subjects.

Chapter 3

Learning from Italy

Petrarchan Sonnets

Sonnets began in Italy in the thirteenth century, and derive their name from the Italian *sonetto*, or 'little sound.' Sicilian poet Giacomo da Lentini is credited with devising the form, and Guittone d'Arezzo for importing it to his native Tuscany, but it was Francesco Petrarca who popularised the pattern, and after whom the Petrarchan sonnet is named.

The fourteen-line form emerged as the perfect vehicle for love poems, lyrics and short narratives. It gives space for a thought to be expressed and considered, but is not long enough to accommodate any wasted words or waffle, or to become tedious. It is challenging to write but not impossible, and has been popular with poets and readers for centuries.

All the lines are written in iambic pentameter. The opening eight lines, the octave, have a set rhyming pattern of: a b b a a b b a, and so use just two rhyming sounds. You will note that this part of the poem consists of two Italian envelopes, using the same rhymes for each. There's an interesting sound effect, too, produced by the four lines in the middle, where the form turns itself inside out to give us: b a a b embedded within an a b b a envelope.

The octave is usually followed by a *volta*, a turn in the middle of the sonnet. There is no strict rule about what happens at the turn. It may denote a shift in viewpoint, the introduction of a new idea, or a new aspect on the theme. The six lines that follow it, the sestet, cannot be described so easily as there are various different structures in place. At first, the sestet rhymed: c d e c d e or c d c c d c, and soon another option was added: c d c d c d.

This Petrarchan sonnet, an example of meta poetry, (poem

written about writing poetry,) demonstrates the standard octave followed by a sestet in the c d e c d e pattern.

ART AND CRAFT

You learn to craft a poem, understand	a
how rhyme and rhythm function as a pair,	b
how metre counts its beat, exactly where	b
to place each stress. You learn that forms demand	a
precise interpretation. Having scanned	a
initial drafts for gross mistakes, you stare	b
at every word and syllable, aware	b
meticulous revision aids your hand.	a
But put aside the theory. All these tricks	c
in use of language may delight the mind	d
of academics. Set your work apart,	e
conjure a touch of magic in the mix;	c
make poems zip and sparkle, and you'll find	d
the craft's pedestrian. You'll learn the art.	e

White space has been left at the turn, to form the poem into two stanzas. This is an optional layout. Some Petrarchan sonnets are written as a single stanza. There is one variant in the metre, where an initial trochaic substitution is found in line 12, opening with a stressed syllable followed by an unstressed one, and then returning to the iambic pattern. There's also an example of dialect affecting rhyme, where full rhyme is dependent on the use of the short -a sound in *demand* rather than a longer, more sustained vowel sound.

Sonnets crossed to England in the sixteenth century, introduced by Thomas Wyatt. His contemporary, the Earl of Surrey, was instrumental in altering their rhyming pattern. By the nature of its construction, the Italian language offers a lot more rhymes for its end sounds than English. The requirement to find two sounds to appear in the octave and offer four rhyming words each, while making perfect sense in the poem, is far more difficult to achieve in English.

The new format, known as the Elizabethan sonnet but often identified by Shakespeare's name, demands just one pair of words for each sound. So seven rhyme sounds are introduced, each of which needs a single rhyme. The pattern is: a b a b c d c d e f e f g g, and the turn appears much later in the poem, before the final rhyming couplet. This means that the summing-up or comment aspect of the piece becomes a punchline, rather than being almost balanced with the opening.

DECEMBER

A scent of Christmas permeates the air	a
in subtle earthy tones of ivy leaves,	b
in holly's prickle and the musk of fir,	a
while aromatic cinnamon spice weaves	b
in fragrances of orange, apple, fig.	c
Where frost has etched a filigree of fern	d
on windows, drawn its rime on branch and twig,	c
its cold, sharp scent pervades. As candles burn	d
their wax exudes an incense, mingles through	e
delicious smells of cooking, warm mince pies,	f
mulled wine and gingerbread. You learn anew	e
the aura of excitement and surprise,	f
and sense, despite the Yule log's cheering glow,	g
December's perfumed promises of snow.	g

The option of indenting the last couplet has been used here. This sonnet, too, can be divided into stanzas if preferred, in the pattern of either twelve lines as the first stanza and the last two as the second, or four lines in each of the first three stanzas, and the final two as the fourth stanza.

While the Elizabethan sonnet has remained fixed, Petrarchan sonnets have seen various adjustments to their sestet under the pens of English poets. These include patterns of: c d e d c e, c d d c d c, c d c d e e, and c d d e c e. All of these rhyme schemes are acceptable.

While many writers have explored and developed sonnets with all kinds of variations on the form, perhaps the most interesting modern variants are those that originated in America. Three notable forms include the Foster sonnet, rhyming: a b c c a a b b d d e e f f, the Mason sonnet: a b c a b c c b d b a d d a, and the Beymorlin sonnet which produces two sets of rhymes throughout the poem. The first rhyme appears within the opening two syllables of each line, and the second at the end, and the Shakespearean pattern is used for both. In this example, the first half of the alphabet is used to indicate the rhymes at the beginning of lines, and the second half for those at the end.

SEEING DAVID HOCKNEY'S: 'A BIGGER SPLASH'

a	Blue water glimmers, mirrored in blue sky	m
b	Where sun, unseen, sends brilliant glow of heat.	n
a	Two palms, unbending, fan green fronds on high.	m
b	Air sweats with August where bright colours meet.	n
c	Reflected shapes make window-image show	o
d	To prove that there is life beyond the frame,	p
c	Expected guests and furnished overflow,	o
d	A moving pattern fixed to forge the game.	p
e	Real motion is the aftermath of plunge.	q
f	A swimmer scythes pool surface. Shooting spray	r
e	Steals rainbows for each crystal. Fountains lunge	q
f	And glimmer, glisten, prismed as they play.	r

g Brash-coloured, angular, bold-stroked and free,   s

g *Splash* reaches from the canvas; drenches me.   S

One point demonstrated here is the use of upper case letters to start each line. This practice, once universal, has fallen out of favour in poetry. Lines seem to flow more naturally if they don't hiccup on a mid-sentence capital letter. Sometimes, however, it seems appropriate to return to the practice for a particular poem. It isn't a question of right or wrong; just a matter of style.

To keep up to date with the latest advances in sonnet writing, you can surf numerous sites that show where today's writers are taking the form. You may invent your own variations to add in; but if you can master both the Petrarchan and the Elizabethan pattern, you will have all the skills of the sonnet at your fingertips.

Ottava Rima

This form was created in Italy during the 1300s, and as its name suggests, it has eight lines. It is the stanza pattern used by Boccaccio in two of his epic poems, and for Byron's *Don Juan*. Poems may have any number of stanzas, and are usually written in iambic pentameters, with the rhyme scheme: a b a b a b c c. This is a good medium for narrative poetry.

BYRON IN VENICE

No traveller who, wearied of the sights   a

his ever-seeking journey shows him, can   b

resist the dream of Venice. From the heights   a

of marble palaces to water's depth, the span   b

connecting land to land, the gaudy nights,   a

there glows a flame to touch the heart of man.   b

So Byron, sickened by the real world, fell   c

beneath the painted city's haunting spell.   c
First drawn by water, he who on the land   d
was clumsy, whose lame foot set him apart,   e
had found the element he could command.   d
Along the cool canals he'd swim, and dart   e
with speed and grace. By night, a torch in hand   d
held high to warn the gondoliers, he'd part   e
the lapping waters. In the day he'd float   f
above them, his reflections for a boat.   f

And love came soon for one whose strong desire   g
was never sated. With his change of scene   h
he found a mistress burning with a fire   g
to match his own, a gipsy-featured queen.   h
Her husband, taking horns for his attire,   g
respected custom, did not intervene   h
to break the match. His baser instincts fed,   i
Lord Byron sought more solace out of bed.   i

By day he joined the holy brotherhood   j
for talk and contemplation, and to learn   k
their tongue. On St. Lazzaro long he stood   j
within the convent garden, or he'd turn   k
his gaze across the water, watch the flood   j
and ebb until the sun had dropped to burn   k
the sea. By night a furious revelry   l
unmasked the remnants of nobility.   l

The glory faded; salons were bedimmed   m
and tricks and pleasures crumbled dry in dust.   n
The poet, weary, unclosed eyes red-rimmed,   m
was conjured more by fear of plague than lust.   n
Dog-days of summer drew his lifeblood, skimmed   m
his dreams away and left a heat-scoured crust;   n

but – oh, had he not seen the city, then   o
the magic would have withered in his pen.   o

Terza Rimas

While the larger part of the Petrarchan sonnet form, and almost the whole of the Elizabethan, count in blocks of four lines, terza rima (third rhyme) is a delightful form focussing on units of three. It, too, comes from Italy.

The form is made up of any number of tercets – stanzas of three lines – followed by a final stanza of either one or two lines. The stanzas are chain-rhymed, so a sound introduced in one stanza is picked up and used in the next, to form a pattern of: a b a b c b c d c d e d e f e f g f etc. The final single line or couplet rhymes with the middle line of the last tercet. Terza rimas are usually written in iambic pentameter.

As far as content is concerned, this is a versatile vehicle. It has the fluency to support a lyrical piece, and can also drive a good narrative. A flippant or a philosophical poem can work as a terza rima, and it can be purely descriptive or action packed.

This example demonstrates the couplet ending.

POSSESSED

I was amazed by magic. She transformed   a
a pumpkin to a carriage, six white mice   b
to horses, and a rat to uniformed   a

and bright-eyed footman. Jewels beyond price   b
gleamed at my throat, my rags became a dress   c
of silk, and, glittering like crystal ice,   b

upon my feet, glass slippers sparked, fluoresced.   /c
I'd heard my Fairy Godmother explain   d
that I must leave by midnight; but, possessed,   /c

those shoes kept waltzing, spinning to the strain	d
of unheard music, forcing me to dance	e
in giddy circles, tipsy with champagne,	d
with wild exhilaration and romance.	e
When midnight chimed they fixed me to the floor	f
and would not let me leave. I took my chance	e
and wrenched them from my feet, raced for the door,	f
leapt out as silk turned rags; as air grew chill	g
they danced on, footless, to some silent score.	f
And now, enchanted, those glass slippers still	g
possess me, twist each movement to their will.	g

A terza rima consisting of fourteen lines - four tercets and a couplet - is also known as a terza rima sonnet, with its turn after the first twelve lines. It's an attractive form to use when you know the content you are planning to put into the poem will divide itself naturally into groups of three lines, or if you are planning to make four separate points before the punchline.

Exercises

13. Think of an idea for a descriptive, atmospheric or narrative poem that could take place on a dark night. Assemble some lists of rhyming words that might be useful, eg. *Night/light/sight/white* and *dark/spark/mark*.

14. Using the same idea, decide on the content you would like to include in the poem, and divide it into appropriate sections. Would it work best as a Petrarchan or Elizabethan sonnet, or a terza rima sonnet? Think of both the weight of content and the placing of the turn. Draft

your sonnet according to your preferred format. If you find it doesn't work, try one of the other patterns.

15. Draft a terza rima involving landscape and weather, but using them as the backdrop for some action rather than a descriptive nature piece. Select the length simply by stopping the tercets when you have said everything you want to communicate. Try out both the single line and couplet endings, to see which is better.

16. Think of a story – a personal anecdote or something you have heard or read before – and convert it into ottava rimas. Put it away for a couple of weeks. Have another look at it. Is the form right for the story? Or could you find a more appropriate form?

17. Take any sonnet written by somebody else, and convert it from Petrarchan to Elizabethan or vice versa, retaining meaning but changing the words to fit into the form's pattern. This is, of course, purely an exercise and not for submission.

18. Write an original love poem as a sonnet or terza rima. Remember that it's all been said before: you need a completely new angle. Let your imagination run riot, considering even the most preposterous approaches. Somewhere there might be one that makes sense... and gives the world a new way to look at love.

Chapter 4

Let's Hear it Again...

Many forms of poetry feature repetitions and refrains. Using the same word, phrase or line more than once gives a lovely enclosed feel to a poem, and imbues a strong sense of poetry – if it is intentional. Unintentional repetition can be the kiss of death.

Let's look at the problem area first. A poem is short and tautly written. There is considerable emphasis on every word. Few people skim-read poetry. Most concentrate on each word and phrase, knowing that extra layers of meaning, interesting wordplay and a lusciousness of sound may appear at any point. A poem that repeats words - other than in a set pattern or to add particular emphasis - does itself no favours. The inference is that the poet was too lazy to look for the best, most exciting use of language, and so resorted to something that was used earlier.

We have already considered the use of identical or very similar rhyming sounds in close proximity. They don't have to be avoided altogether. In a long poem, there is seldom a problem with returning to a rhyme when several different rhymes have intervened since its last appearance. In a short poem, particularly when read aloud, the repeated sound glares.

So much for the bad news. The good news is that intentional repetition supplements the two general benefits listed at the start of this chapter by providing staging posts through the poem, suggesting to readers that they are being guided in the right direction by a confident hand, and adds weight to the message.

Repetition may indicate an obsessive or haunting message, but this is not its only forte. It also possesses a very special aura of reassurance. Repeated phrases are at the heart of our first ever experience of language. Babies are calmed by mini chants of *There, there*, or *Mummy's here*, or *You're such a good boy/girl*.

Repeats feature in nursery rhymes, the first poems many of us learn, as demonstrated at the start of Chapter Two. Think of a few nursery rhymes, and analyse their use of repetition. Transfer the exercise to other poems written for young children.

Adult readers may have given up playing *This little piggy went to market...* with their toes, but they are not immune to the comfort factor of repetition. The following forms all have a long history and are still used today, a good measure of their quality and appeal. Each features elements of repetition that are key to moulding its pattern.

Triolets

If Italy provided a couple of the favourite forms of poetry in the English language, France is responsible for still more, many of which are rooted in the same family. The triolet is a neat little French form, that can sometimes pack a surprising punch to deliver its message.

Triolets are just eight lines long, but as three of them are repeats there are really only five original lines. The rhyme pattern is: A B a A a b A B and the lines are usually written in iambic trimeter, tetrameter or pentameter. Other patterns can be used if preferred, as long as all the lines in the poem have the same metre and length.

The whole line repetition introduces a good question. Should the line generate an identical message each time it is used? Preferably not. In a skilfully crafted poem, the recurrence of a complete line should have a slightly different resonance from the last time it appeared, to show that the poem is moving forward through its content, and is not stuck in a loop. (Of course, if the poem is about being stuck in some constantly repeated situation, it's an advantage to use repetitions in a way that does not move the writing on.)

In this example, the forward motion of the poem attempts to instil a sense of growing revulsion.

GROSS

A cockroach, lurking in my drawer,	A
strolls through my socks and underpants.	B
It freaks me out. It's gross. I roar	a
"A cockroach!" Lurking in my drawer	A
it's had the freedom to explore	a
my secret things. I squirm at *ants*	b
A COCKROACH lurking in my drawer	A
Strolls through my socks and underpants.	B

In this poem, the wording of the repeated lines is unchanged. It is permissible to use just a very little latitude in repeats, the qualifier applied because a drastic change undermines the dynamics of the repetition. There is no problem with changing the grammar and presentation of the lines, though, and in fact this can be a pleasing facet of the poem.

Triolets do not give the scope to analyse the place of man in the universe or recount the storyline of Homer's *Odyssey*, but their brevity is ideal for expressing a brief thought or comment, or for a touch of humour.

Rondels

Dating back to the thirteenth century, the rondel, from the French for 'little round', has thirteen lines arranged in three stanzas, and again features whole-line repetition. The form is a good vehicle for a wide range of subject matter that can be dealt with in a fairly short treatment.

Iambic tetrameter is the favoured metrical form, while the rhyme scheme is: A B b a   a b A B   a b b a A. Some poets like to use an extra syllable, in the form of a feminine ending, for one of the sets of rhymes.

A variant is the rondel supreme, or rondel prime, which has an extra line, to give a pattern of: A B b a   a b A B   a b b a A B.

This gives the effect of both the last stanzas ending with the two lines that opened the poem, which seems to make the piece more complete.

BEACHCOMBING

You find among the tideline's litter	A
a harvest gleaned from storm and loss -	B
a beer can, single sandal, dross,	b
a plastic spade with salt-crust glitter.	a
Where shingles mark the ripples' skitter	a
and foam's a mist of candyfloss,	b
You find among the tideline's litter	A
a harvest gleaned from storm and loss;	B
and seagulls' screech and dunlins' twitter	a
make mournful music. Wavelets toss	b
this scrapped, sad history scrawled across	b
dead summer's face. The wind blows bitter.	a
You find among the tideline's litter	A
a harvest gleaned from storm and loss	B

Line 11 illustrates a point that's worth considering when you are writing in a strict metre. There are many words that can occupy different numbers of syllables, according to the way they are pronounced. This example presupposes that *history* is pronounced as *hist'ry*, and so reads as two syllables rather than three. A triphthong, where three separate vowel sounds are amalgamated into one, permits the same flexibility. So words like *fire* and *power*, although correctly pronounced as a single syllable, can be read as two. These quirky variants of pronunciation add an interesting touch to metre. Sometimes they work, sometimes not: but they are another tool in the kit.

Don't forget that even when whole lines recur, there is still a challenge to find appropriate rhymes to fit amongst them. The longer the form, the more rhymes you will need. Do bear this in mind from the start. It isn't enough to avoid using *pint* and *film* as your line end words; think around a vocabulary that will present you with rhyming options that are likely to fit into the poem you are planning, and you will find the task of writing much easier.

Chaucerian Roundels

Just two lines longer than the triolet, and developed via the rondel, the Chaucerian roundel – popularised, unsurprisingly, by Geoffrey Chaucer – has ten lines rhyming: A b b   a b A   a b b A. So the opening, repeated line appears at the mid point and at the end of the poem. It is usually written in iambic tetrameters or pentameters.

This is another form whose length requires a little cameo of an idea, a fragment rather than a complete argument, but which can be surprisingly memorable.

ERROR REPORT

I wish I could erase mistakes	A
made in my rather foolish past;	b
I never realised shame would last	b
so long, or that its shadow breaks	a
the most confirmed iconoclast.	b
I wish I could erase mistakes.	A

My built-on-sand life shudders, shakes   a
and crashes down. And I am cast   b
as failure, useless and outclassed.   b
I wish I could erase mistakes.   A

Rondeaus

The repetition in this three-stanza form is much lighter than the ones we have looked at, because it involves only a portion of a line rather than the whole one. It may be as brief as a single word, or consist of a more substantial phrase, but is always shorter than a line. Its echoing quality combined with its comparative brevity leaves a wisp of music in the reader's ear. Whatever your subject matter, you will find that the refrain leaves an impression, so choose it with care.

This refrain opens the poem and ends the two final stanzas. The rhyme structure is: R:a a b b a   a a b R   a a b b a R, and again iambic feet are used, in tetrameters or pentameters.

GUEST SPEAKER

All smiles, she greets the Chairman at the door,   R:a
and overwhelms him with her dulcet roar: a
takes off her coat, decides to keep the hat -   b
(ridiculous confection) - orders that   b
they bring her coffee, cake and petits-fours.   a

Before she speaks, she wants to be quite sure   a
the audience will know - and be in awe -   a
of who she is. She gives this caveat,   b
    all smiles.   R

She condescends to glance around the floor,   a
then patronises for an hour or more.   a
Because she's such a grand aristocrat   b

(she tells the Chairman) she won't stay to chat.	b
She takes her fee, sails down the corridor …	a
all smiles.	R

The raison d'être of this poem, incidentally, is revenge, exposing an appalling speaker who traded shamelessly on her name but had no qualms about accepting a large cheque. Writing a poem like this is a pleasing way of getting even, and as long as your subject is not named or recognisable, no-one can touch you for it.

Roundels

In the nineteenth century, Swinburne adapted the rondeau form to create the shorter eleven line roundel. He retained the use of the opening phrase or word as a refrain which appears as line 4 and as the final line, and built in the option that the refrain may rhyme if you so wish. Any single line length and metre can be used, and the form is usually applied to lyric poetry.

This pattern also has two rhyming sounds. If the refrain does not rhyme, the scheme is: a b a R   b a b   a b a R. With rhyme, this becomes: R(B):a b a R(B)   b a b   a b a R(B) showing that the refrain rhymes with the second line. Here's an example of the rhymed refrain version.

STREET STATUES, BARCELONA

A neverending show; each actor stands	R(B):a
until the tourists snap, and then a flow	b
of fluid motion drifts. This work commands	a
a neverending show.	R(B)

Heat scorches through the harsh metallic glow	b
of bronze, gold, silver make-up, and leaves brands	a
of pain on nerve and muscle. When the slow	b

siesta hours have turned to evening, tanned /a
sunseekers make for bars. The actors go b
to soak pale skin and sleep. Next day demands a
  a neverending show. R(B)

Kyrielle

This French medieval form is based on part of the church liturgy, the responsive *Kyrie, eleison*. It is written in any number of quatrains, but the fact that the refrain which occurs in each needs a rhyme may inhibit the number of stanzas included.

Iambic tetrameter is the most popular metre for this form, which is seen in a number of hymns as well as in poetry. Each stanza may consist of two rhymed couplets, or alternate rhyming lines, to give the pattern: a a b B   c c b B   d d b B   e e b B   or a b a B   c b c B   d b d B   e b e B.

Kyrielles often have a devotional theme, but this is not compulsory, as the irreverent example shows. Modern ones may demonstrate slight variations in the repeats.

A MINOR CASE OF HEDONISM

Days crammed with odds-and-ends to do a

like groundhog moments, déjà vu, a
allow no time to wallow in; b
sit back, and feel the planet spin. B

For leisure seems a luxury c
that's too benign for you and me. c
Indulgence? Or a hint of sin? b
Sit back, and feel the planet spin. B

We'll talk of this and talk of that	d
and spend an hour in idle chat,	d
but know we're wasting time. We grin,	b
sit back and feel the planet spin.	B

And when the housework isn't done	e
we just acknowledge it's more fun	e
to laugh and let good times to begin -	b
sit back and feel the planet spin.	B

For we exult in Davies' scheme	f
to stand and stare all day, and dream,	f
to give up work, to pour a gin,	b
sit back and feel the planet spin.	B

This form occasionally appears in a couplet version, rhyming: a A   a A   a A   a A etc. Unsurprisingly, this is a lot less popular than the quatrain stanzas, with both readers and writers.

Ballades

These medieval French poems, too, seem to be designed to test rhyming skills to the limits, and because of the way the language rhymes, are more difficult to write in English than in French. They are twenty-eight lines long, made up of three eight-line stanzas and a shorter envoi, and most are written in iambic tetrameter or pentameter. The last line of the first stanza recurs as a refrain.

Only three rhyming sounds are used throughout, which means it is important to find rhymes that give you plenty of options. The spread is uneven, so do bear this in mind when making your selections. The second sound, b, requires fourteen words that rhyme together and will make sense in a poem. The first rhyme sound, a, needs six words, while the third sound, c, only needs five in view of the refrains. There is something gripping about the form, so while it can be used for landscape poems, it is also a good vehicle for highly emotional pieces. The pattern is: a b a b b c b C   a b a b b c b C   a b a b b c b C   b c b C.

WHO NEEDS A FRIEND?

The party is a huge success,	a
good food, good music, folk who may	b
be friends. I offer my address,	a
suggest they come to me one day.	b
Now all my fears that I would stay	b
a stranger here have flown. I think	c
I like this neighbourhood, and say	b
perhaps I'll have just one more drink.	C

Time passes, and I must confess,	a
I've lost touch with my friends. Today	b
I'll call them up. I'll buy a dress,	a
and food and wine without delay,	b
and hang some decorations. They	b
will all be here. I used to shrink	c
from crowds; but no more. Anyway,	b
perhaps I'll have just one more drink.	C

It was a shame no one said yes.	a
I've heaps of food. I think I'll play	b
some music – fill the emptiness	a
and keep the lonely thoughts at bay.	b
I take a tumbler from the tray.	b
The bottles catch the light and wink.	c
I drain the glass. My mood is grey.	b
Perhaps I'll have just one more drink.	C

Who needs a friend? A liquid way	b
will carry me beyond the brink.	c
Today's no worse than yesterday.	b
Perhaps I'll have just one more drink.	C

The ballade supreme is longer, but allows you an extra rhyming sound. This has thirty-five lines divided into three ten line stanzas and a five line envoi. Its pattern is: a b a b b c c d c D   a b a b b c c d c D   a b a b b c c d c D   c c d c D

A complete poem taking the same pattern as one of the ballade's eight line stanzas is known as a huitain, and a complete poem with the same pattern as the ballade supreme's ten line stanza is a dizain – considered in more detail in the next chapter.

Villanelles

Originally a work-song for French farm labourers in the Middle Ages, the villanelle has been adapted to become a popular form to write, and an attractive one to hear. The most frequently quoted example of the form – and rightly so, because it's a wonderful poem – is *Do Not Go Gentle into that Good Night* by Dylan Thomas.

There are two refrain lines, but unlike the poems we have looked at so far, they rhyme together rather than using different sounds. The bulk of the poem is made up of tercets, and the two refrains first appear as the first and third lines of the opening tercet. Thereafter they take it in turns to recur as the final line of each tercet. The last stanza is a quatrain, ending with both the refrains. There may be any odd number of tercets followed by the quatrain, but poets generally gravitate towards an overall length of nineteen lines. This is enough to establish the message of a poem, but prevents the work from becoming tedious through over-use of refrains.

In each tercet, the opening line rhymes with the refrain, and all the middle lines rhyme together. This produces a rhyme scheme: A1 b A2   a b A1   a b A2   a b A1   a b A2   a b A1 A2. Iambic pentameters or tetrameters are used.

Villanelles can be written on any subject, but the quantity of repetition gives the poem a haunted atmosphere. This makes it ideally suited to obsessive themes, a recurring situation, a repeated action, etc.

AFTERMATH

My mistress seems distracted, gives commands	A1
that make no sense. She cries of blood. All day	b
she paces back and forth and wrings her hands.	A2
It all began that time the king, his bands	a
of followers, attendants came to stay.	b
My mistress seems distracted, gives commands	A1
then contradicts them, makes absurd demands.	a
She talks of witches' promises. The way	b
she paces back and forth and wrings her hands	A2
makes doctors, servants, all her household brand	/a
her crazed, insane; but no-one will betray	b
their mistress. She, distracted, gives commands	A1
and each of us pretends to understand	/a
her garbled talk of letters, Duncan slain.	/b
She paces back and forth and wrings her hands.	A2
The thane has gone. His titles, castle, lands	a
mean nothing now; and, too disturbed to pray,	b
my mistress is distracted, gives commands.	A1
She paces back and forth and wrings her hands.	A2

This villanelle demonstrates three points. First, we've seen before how a slight difference in rhyming sounds can work without any problems, and indeed can offer a pleasing effect. It's up to both poet and reader to decide whether such adjustments work well or simply sound wrong. The clue is in the word 'sound.' The poem may be heard at a reading, or if it is studied from the page, the sound of the words chimes in the reader's mind. To check how effective any quirk of rhyming is, the best technique is to read the piece aloud. If it sounds fine, it is. If you, its author, feel that it involves too much compromise, then it does, and the rest of the world will feel the same. The differences here, with the use of *brand* and *understand*, where the final *s* is lost in order to furnish the correct verb form, and the *n* added to the second rhyming sound to form *slain*, seem appropriate. Do you agree? Some readers will, some won't.

Secondly, it is acceptable in a villanelle to make slight changes in the wording of the refrains, in order to make sense in the poem while keeping the impetus going. The last line of the fourth stanza here shows such a variant. It has been kept as close as possible to the original, with the changing of just two words. The substitution of *their* for *my* at the start of the line slips past quite easily, because it is on an unstressed syllable. The use of *She* replacing *seems* falls on a stressed syllable, and therefore stands out more. In order to minimise the difference, the same vowel appears in each word, so there is strong similarity of sound. Again, both writer and reader have to be happy about any adjustments, so it's up to the poet to ensure that they are slight enough to be accepted by most readers.

The final point concerns grammar, punctuation and sentence structuring. Making adjustments to these factors - without compromising the wording in any way - is once more encouraged. It provides both variety and fascination for the reader, and is a fun exercise for the writer.

One extra hint: when you embark on writing a villanelle,

don't forget that the first and third lines of the poem must appear consecutively in the last stanza. Be sure they will make sense when placed together. There's a lot of work to undo if there is no way they will form a logical couplet.

Pantoums

You may have noticed that every form we have looked at so far uses only two rhyming sounds to create its effect. With pantoums we have a lot more rhymes – for good reason. Every single line in the poem appears twice in its entirety. With such swathes of repetition, the variety provided by a range of rhymes is essential, particularly if you want the audience to stay awake while you read it.

This is a Malayan form, brought to Europe in the 1820s, and a form where you have to be careful that the cleverness of the pattern does not dominate, and the message of the poem is allowed to come through. The need to keep the content moving forward, even though the last line of the poem is the same as the first, should be borne in mind throughout the writing process.

If the villanelle is a vehicle for obsessive themes, the pantoum takes it up a notch and lends itself to the totally compulsive, urgent, emotionally charged material. Remember, like all other set forms, pantoums can be written on any subject; but when you are matching theme to form, the inner nature of the form remains a good guideline.

Pantoums are written in any number of quatrains, usually in iambic pentameter or tetrameter. There are rhymes in the first and third lines of each stanza, and in the second and fourth. The stanzas interlock, and the second and fourth lines of each stanza become the first and third of the next. At the end of the poem, its first and third lines appear in the final stanza, but in reverse order. A variant is to end the poem with a couplet consisting of the first and third lines, again in reverse order.

The pattern is: A1 B1 A2 B2   B1 C1 B2 C2   C1 D1 C2 D2   D1

E1 D2 E2 and then the final stanzas: Y1 Z1 Y2 Z2 Z1 A2 Z2 A1
or: Y1 Z1 Y2 Z2 A2 A1. Remember, Y and Z could be any letters
- you don't have to write twenty-six stanzas. In fact, with all that
repetition, it's much better if you don't.

UNDERFOOT

No compromise for Pharaohs. Only gold	A1
was rich enough embellishment to blaze	B1
on jewellery, clothing, shoes. Now sterile, cold,	A2
great Tutankhamen's chattels still amaze	B2
in rich enough embellishment. To blaze	B1
his message, craftsmen laboured hour on hour -	C1
(great Tutankhamen's chattels still amaze) -	B2
made gem-starred chests and thrones to prove his power.	C2
His message: craftsmen laboured hour on hour	C1
to show how standing still is mere defeat;	D1
made gem-starred chests and thrones to prove his power,	C2
and fixed his enemies beneath his feet.	D2
To show how standing still is mere defeat	D1
they made his sandals icons, took gold thread	E1
and fixed his enemies beneath his feet	D2
by drawing them where sole and heel would tread.	E2
They made his sandals icons; took gold thread,	E1
stitched images of foes that he could quell	F1
by drawing them where sole and heel would tread,	E2
(humiliation worse for them than hell.)	F2

Stitched images of foes that he could quell   F1
were crushed by time, each victory turned to dross -   G1
humiliation worse for them than hell -   F2
when mighty kingdoms crumbled into dust./   G2

Where crushed by time, each victory turned to dross   G1
on jewellery, clothing, shoes - now sterile, cold.   A2
When mighty kingdoms crumbled into dust,/   G2
no compromise: for Pharaohs, only gold.   A1

This example indicates again how sentence structuring can be adjusted without altering the wording, to keep the integrity of the form and yet still ring the changes.

Sestinas

If a pantoum presents a puzzle, a sestina turns the knife. This form, which started life among twelfth century French troubadours, is as much a mathematical puzzle as a type of poem. It has thirty-nine lines divided into six stanzas of six lines each, and an envoi of three lines at the end. That sounds simple enough, but is complicated by the fact that you use the same six words at the line ends of every stanza, in a different, strictly calculated order, so that each word appears in every possible position. Then for good measure, the six words are all brought together in the envoi, one used internally and the other at the end of each line, again in a set pattern.

Although sestinas tend to be written in iambic metre and with lines of equal length, some modern sestinas are not bound to a particular metre. The line end pattern is: A B C D E F   F A E B D C   C F D A B E   E C B F A D   D E A C F B   B D F E C A   B:E D:C F:A.

Sestinas are not always the best form to use for a narrative poem, though there have been notable exceptions, but once more there is a feeling of a compulsive nature in the structure. This sestina takes the same general theme as the pantoum we looked at, but brings Ancient Egypt into the realms of today's tourists rather than the shoemakers of the fourteenth century BC.

UPPER EGYPT

A strip of blessing cleaving desert sand,	A
the Nile flows as it has for ages past,	B
its banks a fertile haven, bringing life	C
to barren ground, while unrelenting sun	D
bakes mud bricks, bleaches rock and scorches stone.	E
The very air vibrates with legend, tales	F
of pharaohs and their queens, of gods, those tales	F
that whisper through the night in sifting sand.	A
More solid are the histories in stone	E
where chiselled scenes and hieroglyphs have passed	B
their culture, folklore, father down to son,	D
their glory moments, and their daily life.	C
Now poverty and politics make life	C
a struggle to exist, and only tales	F
that lure expectant tourists seeking sun	D
provide a way to eke a wage from sand.	A
So beads, papyri, perfumes sell, the past	B
reduced to trinkets, scarabs carved in stone.	E
The list of must-see sites is set in stone,	E
where Luxor's temple demonstrates a life	C
of unremitting faith, where pharaohs passed	B
from east to west bank's hidden tombs, with tales	F
of Nefertiti, Tutankhamen, sand	A
and dust, Nile's ripples glinting in the sun.	D

At last, a long straight drive while dawning sun	D
ignites the desert, and there soars the stone	E
great Rameses erected in the sand	A
as temples, massive effigies, a life	C
encapsulated, spawning vaunting tales	F
so Nubians would honour Egypt's past.	B

And up and down the river, ships glide past	B
fields, donkeys, villages and palm trees, sun	D
ubiquitous as much-repeated tales.	F
Civilisation summarised in stone	E
becomes a monument to show that life	C
is nothing more than breeze-blown grains of sand.	A

Rich echoes of the past, preserved in stone,	B:E
burn stronger than the sun, while mortal life	D:C
evaporates like tales borne in the sand.	F:A

A useful trick in the sestina is to find words with more than one meaning, to extend the possibilities for variety, or use homophones such as *sun/son* and *past/passed*.

You will see that there's no rhyme in the line endings of this poem, but you can also write a rhymed sestina. Just to keep poets on their toes, the rhymed sestina works on the same principle, but has a different order of the line end sounds, with: A1 B1 A2 B2 A3 B3   B3 A1 B2 A2 B1 A3   A3 B3 A1 B2 A2 B1   B1 A3 B3 A1 B2 A2   A2 B1 A1 B3 A3 B2   B2 A2 B1 A3 B3 A1   A1:B2 B1:A2 A3:B3. In order to avoid rhyming couplets occurring in this form, the change of line end word order means that there is some duplication of position, such as the placing of the poem's first line as its third, both in stanzas 3 and 5.

This poem shows how the rhyme scheme is fitted in. Saying it aloud gives a good sense of the effect of its rhyming.

HAUNTED

Be careful walking through the woods at night.	A1
The paths are winding, difficult by day	B1
and treacherous in evening's fading light.	A2
As leaf and sky and fern all merge in grey	B2
and trees cast shadows on the edge of sight,	A3
perhaps it would be wise to run away.	B3
When squirrels, rabbits, mice have crept away	B3
the woods are left to creatures of the night,	A1
to foxes slinking low to earth, and grey	B2
outlines of bat and owl, while dwindling light	A2
extinguishes the final beams of day,	B1
and hints of cheer and warmth sink out of sight.	A3
An ancient legend tells this is the site	A3
where highwaymen and cutthroats hid away,	B3
and yet the unforgiving cloak of night	A1
lifted enough for vague shapes, spectral grey,	B2
to be discovered, hanged at dawn's first light	A2
and quartered in the early hours of day.	B1
And from that time, despite the dawning day,	B1
their ghosts materialise, and in plain sight	A3
they lumber through the trees. To race away	B3
is hopeless, for they grow, and black as night	A1
they loom above, around you, while a grey,	B2
foul-smelling haze saps all the good from light.	A2
They feed on fear, and any speck of light	A2
that could empower you is snuffed out, so day	B1
- its hope and promise poisoned by the night -	A1
becomes a source of terror, drives away	B3

your practical beliefs until your sight   A3
is compromised, and all the world is grey   B2

and hideous monstrosities. When grey   B2
at last displaces black, when rays of light   A2
insinuate the rationale of day   B1
to calm your terrors, you will find your sight   A3
will be forever changed, disturbed. Away   B3
from haunted paths, your dreams will rage the night. A1

For in these woods, when deep night pales to grey, A1:B2
the tainted shreds of day shed toxic light   B1:A2
corrupting sight. It's best to run away.   A3:B3

Exercises

19. Think back to schooldays. Remember all your playground games that involved repetition. Try crafting a triolet about one. Now try a rondel or Chaucerian roundel, either about the same game or prompted by another idea on your list. As an added complication, see if you can inject some fragment of mature wisdom into the childhood themed piece, not forgetting that you have very few lines to play with.

20. Explore the rondeau form, starting with the theme of a party. It helps to select the reason it is being held, (eg. wedding reception, or barbecue because the sun's shining,) the style of the party, and the people who are involved. You will also need to decide the voice of the poem's narrator, who could be an individual guest or host, a barman, a spectator with an overview of events, etc. Now think of the word or phrase that will be able to open the poem and also close its second and final stanzas effectively. Write the rondeau.

21. Consider the sort of themes that would work well in the villanelle form. When you have a short list of ideas, devise - as a rhyming couplet - the pair of repeated lines you would use for each. Construct a villanelle using the couplet that appeals to you the most.

22. Think of a theme that keeps niggling at your peace of mind. It could be massive or relatively trivial, of personal or political concern. Develop it in the form of a pantoum, remembering that the first line of the poem will be repeated at the end.

23. Write the first stanza of a sestina, rhymed or unrhymed, with line end words that you could envisage using six more times in the poem, for the five additional stanzas and the envoi. If you like the idea of the challenge this form presents, try a second stanza and possibly complete the poem. Remember to follow the appropriate sequence, depending on your choice of rhymed or unrhymed lines.

24. Think about the ballade. What sort of subject would you be likely to choose to suit the form? Could you find enough words that might fit in with your subject matter and satisfy the requirement of fourteen rhymes for the second sound?

25. What sort of theme would you use in a kyrielle? What would be the refrain? Could you write a kyrielle whose content moves forward in each stanza, so that the refrain has a slightly different resonance each time it is used?

Chapter 5

And Another Thing...

We have looked at couplets, tercets and quatrains, Italian-based poems and poems that rely on repetition, but there are plenty of other styles and devices at the heart of poetry. In this chapter we'll consider another dozen verse forms selected at random, with the reminder that new patterns are emerging all the time. You can keep up to date with them by checking out literary magazines for the appearance of new forms, and watching for them on the internet.

English Odes

Although the word 'ode' has come to be used for any type of poem, it was originally the name of a set form; or rather, of a group of forms dating back to ancient Greece. We'll look at just one version of it. The English, or Keatsian, ode has three stanzas of ten lines each, and is written in iambic pentameters.

The subject matter is traditionally a lyric poem that addresses a person, situation, event, relationship or whatever, with a celebratory note.

The rhyme pattern is: a b a b c d e c d e and each stanza uses the same pattern, but with different rhyming sounds. Although the form of the English ode is quite different from that of a sonnet, it's interesting that it takes the rhyme system of the first four lines of an Elizabethan sonnet, and follows them with one of the versions of the Petrarchan sonnet's sestet.

TO MUSIC

We taste anticipation in the hall.	a
The players finish tuning instruments	b

as the conductor enters. We are all	a
collaborators in the moment, tense	/b
before the baton's raised; and one pure note	c
pervades the silence. Then a rich cascade	d
of chord on chord, of scale on scale bursts forth,	e
transporting us away to drift afloat	c
on streams of sound where sorcery is made,	d
and lifting us above the bounds of earth.	/e

Each bar, each trill, each phrase confirms the proof	f
that through his music, man can take his place	g
an inch below the angels, and this truth	/f
is evident when melodies retrace	g
the routes and joys of living, speaking deep	h
into humanity. The ear, the heart,	i
the mind respond to harmonies that share	j
a promise of enrichment, gifts to keep	h
and treasure when the music stops, their art	i
a talisman more bright than gold, more rare.	j

The last notes fade; vibrations slow and pause,	k

and then a moment's silence forms an arch	l
between the music's end and wild applause.	k
That second grasps the magic, is the charge	/l
to animate responses from the crowd,	m
musicians, from the very air that breathes	n
where music's vibrant power exerts its hold.	o
And there, and in that moment, clear and loud,	m
the music's spirit fills the hall, sings, weaves	n
a thread that dances wild and uncontrolled.	o

This ode includes numerous examples of internal full rhymes, repetition and slant rhymes. These are not a prerequisite, but add a certain grace to the language. Here they also help to reinforce the theme.

Dizains

This French form, the longer stanza of a ballade supreme, has ten lines, and is enclosed and tautly constructed. It lends itself to lyric poetry, and uses iambic tetrameter or pentameter. The rhyme scheme is: a b a b b c c d c d. The pattern suggests a mirror image of sound, and is a good alternative to the sonnet when you are trying to express a brief reflection or short narrative. You can take advantage of the rhyme mirror by creating a turn at the half way point, and giving a shift of subject, emphasis or angle in the last five lines.

SEA CHANGE

It was a perfect day of sea,	a
where sun warmed brine and flecked the land,	b
and seaweed threads made filigree	a
of charcoal shadows. Breezes fanned	b
foam crests to ripple saffron sand.	b
First clouds were hardly noticed, dropped	c
their rain to kiss the shore. Wind cropped	c
the marram grass, whipped waves whose swell	d
turned foam to breakers, overtopped	c
small boats, turned idyll into hell.	d

Kennings

Kennings are a fun form, based on the idea of describing something without actually saying what it is. They are based on old Norse languages, and consist of a list of brief phrases of description – usually consisting of two words, but with plenty of latitude for variation – which all describe elements of the character or item under consideration. They often rhyme, but rhyming is not compulsory.

Sometimes kennings become a riddle, by leaving the reader to work out what the subject is. In this case, the poem begins with the most obscure definitions, and then goes on to more obvious clues. The example given below leaves nothing to chance, as the title explains.

REINDEER KENNING

carrot cruncher
sweet hay muncher
antler wearer
Santa bearer
swoop and soarer
sky explorer
red-nosed racer
moonbeam chaser
sleighbell ringer
big sack bringer
roof tile clatterer
stardust scatterer

The absence of punctuation, capital letters and sentence structuring is not specifically required by the form, but sometimes seems appropriate for the dynamics of the kenning.

Burns Stanza

The Scottish standard habbie form, named after the sixteenth century piper Habbie Simpson, whose death prompted Robert Sempill to write a lament in the form, is also known as the Burns stanza, Scottish stanza or six line stave.

Lines 1, 2, 3 and 5 rhyme together and are written in iambic tetrameters. Lines 4 and 6 rhyme, and are just half the length, written in iambic dimeters. So the rhyme scheme is: a a a b a b.

SEPTUPLETS

Beside the bank, at water's edge,	a
a coot has nested in the sedge	a
in twigs she's woven on a ledge.	a
With high-pitched cheep	b
her seven babies, newly fledged,	a
attempt the leap.	b

As one is chivvied to the nest	c
another tries the daring test,	c
while Mum swims round them, does her best,	c
rounds up her brood,	d
resumes her neverending quest -	c
the search for food.	d

Centos

You don't so much write a cento as compile it. It consists of a mash-up of lines from other poems by one or many other writers, but rearranged into a new order to communicate a new message. It's an ancient form, having been around since the days of ancient Greece, which was popularised in the 300s AD, when centos were constructed from Virgil's work.

Putting together a cento begins with the delightful task of reading all the poems you can find, trawling them for lines you'd like to use. You can make the task easier by copying out each individual line on a separate slip of paper and then shuffling them into different orders. Every line's author should be acknowledged, either beside the individual lines or in a footnote, so a cento writer is not seen as a plagiarist. If you keep to poems which are out of copyright, whose authors have been dead for at least seventy years, you will not risk falling foul of the copyright laws.

This cento has been assembled from the work of nineteenth century poets, and appears as blank verse (see below). Neither of these is a demand of the form, just the compiler's whim.

SHELL OF PEACE

Ah, sad and strange as in dark summer	
dawns	Tennyson
When I have fears that I may cease to be	Keats
I'll walk where my own nature would be	
leading.	C. Bronte
We mortals cross the ocean of this world	R. Browning
Surprised by joy – impatient as the wind.	Wordsworth
Unto thine ear I hold the dead-sea shell	
Of that winged Peace which lulls the breath	
of sighs.	D. G. Rossetti
Remember me when I am gone away,	C. Rossetti
Think but one thought of me up in the stars,	Morris
That light whose smile kindles the universe;	Shelley
But love me for love's sake, that evermore	
Thou may'st love on through love's eternity.	E. B. Browning

Over the years, numerous different approaches have been applied to the cento. These are the main ones:

- Lines written by the compiler may appear, and this is also known as a collage cento.
- Only a single line by another poet is included in your own poem, recurring as a refrain, eg. at the beginning of each stanza.

- Only full lines should be used.
- Shorter and longer extracts could be used.
- Compilers could make tiny changes to the wording, eg. the form of a verb.

Sapphics

Sapphic stanzas are unrhymed quatrains with a strict metrical pattern, and a useful device for communicating lyric and descriptive subjects.

The first three lines of five feet each consist of two trochees, a dactyl and another two trochees. The last line just has two feet, a dactyl and a trochee. This means that the usual advice to start every line with an unstressed syllable is reversed, and each line of the poem needs to start with a stressed syllable.

Stanzas from RAVELLO

Curving road winds up from Amalfi's clamour
where the silent heights drowse in noonday sunshine.
Wide piazza shimmers, and tree-fringed pathways
glint in a heat haze.

Only signs of life are an old man sleeping
shaded by an olive tree, gnarled as he is,
lone dog sniffing scraps, and a black-clad woman
sweeping her shop front.

Stand beneath the palms, let sun-fingers stroke you.
Hear cicadas drown distant drone of traffic.
Breathe in orange fragrance and scent of lemon,
tangy and breeze borne.

Minutes

An American form, the minute is made up of sixty syllables in twelve lines. While these numbers are already hinting at a time reference, another important factor prompted by the name is that the action described in the poem should take place in the space of a minute.

The poem is written in rhyming couplets, making the pattern: a a b b c c d d e e f f, and in strict iambic metre. There are eight syllables in the first, fifth and ninth lines, creating iambic tetrameters, and four syllables in each of the rest, to form iambic dimeters. A further demand of the form is that traditional punctuation and grammar should be applied with accuracy, with capital letters to open new sentences, but not at the beginning of any other line.

LEAVE TAKING

I look into your eyes and know	a
it's time to go,	a
but cannot bear	b
to leave you there.	b
You're old and ill and so afraid,	c
and I've delayed,	c
but now I stand	d
and loose your hand.	d
I kiss your cheek and turn away -	e
wish I could stay.	e
I leave; and sigh	f
a last goodbye.	f

The hardest part of this form is to select an activity that happens within a minute. Once you have done this, the writing is easy. Well, comparatively easy.

Terzanelles

Did you mutter *easy-peasy* as you read about terza rimas and villanelles? If you did, this hybrid form from France and Italy might be just what you need. It does, however, come with a government health warning. Attempting it can cause severe bouts of frustration and sufferers are prone to throwing their laptop through the window. If you still want to try, you will need to write nineteen lines, and although iambic tetrameter and pentameter are the favoured forms, you may use any metre and line length as long as they are the same for each line of the poem.

Considering the rhyme scheme is the best way of seeing how the parent forms have been amalgamated: A1 B A2 b C B c D C d E D e F E f A1 F A2 OR f F A1 A2

PRESENCE

A presence clings to mortar, wood and stone -	A1
old houses know the resonance of years.	B
When you're indoors, you're never on your own.	A2
A wraith of being – not quite soul – adheres	b
to walls that hold remembered breath exhaled	C
in houses. Know the resonance of years	B
where flesh and bone are echoes, weakened, paled	c
by time and inrush of the people who	D
learn walls that hold remembered breath. Exhaled	C
are ghosts of yesterday we never knew,	d
and yet their lives are fused in place with ours	E
by time. An inrush of the people who	D

have made their home here lingers, heightens, flowers.	e
Their essence will console and cheer, enthrall	F
because their lives are fused in place with ours.	E

These spirits of the house sustain us all;	f
their essence will console and cheer, enthrall.	F
A presence clings to mortar, wood and stone -	A1
When you're indoors, you're never on your own.	A2

Once again, we see how easily the sense of a line can be changed by altering the punctuation, or by a little tweak to the wording. The important point about this practice is 'little tweak.' If, instead, it is 'massive alteration,' the dynamic of the form is lost.

You can write terzanelles on any subject, but always remember that the first and third lines of the poem will appear together or with just one other line between them, at the end of the poem. Not only must they make sense in the context, but it must be clear that the poem's message has moved on and not remained static.

Riddles

These ancient poems pre-date written history, and seem to have been used in every country and every culture. In some they were used to communicate information and folklore from generation to generation. They are a sub-genre of didactic or instructional poetry, fascinating to construct and fun to solve.

Generally untitled, riddles may be based on short puns, but verse riddles tend to require a solution that needs lateral thinking. This is a typical example, and just in case you have a problem with it, the answer is at the end of this chapter's exercises.

My first is in water, but isn't in air,
My second's in ocean and sea, but not there.

My third's in a river but not in a vale,
My fourth is in stream, but not moor, hill or dale.
My fifth can be seen in a ditch – not a street -
And my whole can be found under everyone's feet.

Blank Verse

One of the biggest misapprehensions in poetry is that blank verse and free verse are the same. Free verse is a massive topic and will be dealt with in chapter seven. Blank verse can be summed up in three words: unrhymed iambic pentameter.

Blank verse is the poetic language of Shakespeare's plays. Interestingly, it is spoken by his educated and court characters, while the lower ranks in society use prose, and supernatural beings are inclined to rhyme. You will see blank verse in Wordsworth's great poem, *The Prelude*, Tennyson's *Ulysses*, and Milton's *Paradise Lost*.

As soon as you start writing blank verse, you find that its beat is insistent and easy to sustain. Provided that you use an occasional variant to break the monotony, but avoid too many deviations from the form, you can create a vibrant blank verse poem.

This is a brilliant medium for narrative poetry, and adaptable enough to work for verse monologues, and lyric, epic and descriptive poetry. The example below places a monologue in the voice of Shakespeare's fairy queen, Titania.

HELL HATH NO FURY

He thinks that I've capitulated; joke!
When Moth and Cobweb told me what he'd done -
bewitching me, queen of the fairy world,
with drops of love-in-idleness - I knew
that I could work it to my own advantage.   5
He made a fool of me, I'll not deny,

but he won't do it twice. For I'm resolved
to learn those skills that mortal women have,
to flirt and tease, cajole and flatter, charm
until he is besotted. Then I'll turn   10
my back, ignore his wheedling kisses, mock
his efforts to make love to me, and laugh
his macho image into scorn. He thinks
it sport to pair me with a braying ass,
a yokel weaver? Well, we'll see who laughs   15
the last and longest. One thing I have learned:
the bedchamber can make such fools of men,
and he's no better than mere mortals. I'll
inflame his want until he's sick with lust,
and begging for my favours. Then I'll seize   20
my darling changeling boy, escape with him
into the forest's welcoming embrace;
and from a distance watch him, curse him, tell
his dalliance with that horse-faced Amazon
to all the subjects of his fairy kingdom.   25
And when he's on his knees I'll make my move,
return in triumph, take my rightful place
upon his throne - and watch him hit rock bottom.

This poem includes some of the regular variants, such as the
initial trochaic substitution in line 22 and the feminine endings at
the end of lines 5 and 25, and on the dire pun of line 28. You will
also see that there is a mid-line movement away from the regular
iambs in line 3, where the third foot, at the centre of the line, is
turned to form a trochee. This non-standard variant is intended
to draw attention to itself, ensuring that the reader or listener is
perfectly aware of the speaker's identity, and of her own appreciation of her status. So a dramatic element can be added to the
reasons for varying strict form.

Acrostics

Acrostics are lighthearted and fun to create, popular with both adult and child readers, and introduce the gentlest of puzzles. The only requirement of the standard form is that the opening letters of the lines, when read from top to bottom, make up a word or phrase, usually connected with the content of the poem.

Acrostics often rhyme, but they don't have to. They may have metre and equal line lengths, but again you have a choice. This one takes the form of an Elizabethan sonnet, and is about a group of poets known as ... (read the acrostic.)

GATHERING

Away from home, a clutch of poets meet,	a
Cavorting in the Yorkshire countryside	b
Communing with the Muse, or reading sweet,	a
Enduring verse. Discussion ranges wide;	b
New writing springs from first draft to the page.	c
They share the information each has brought,	d
Or study longer works, or they engage	c
Nerve-tingling images as sleek as thought.	d
Pens sheathed, they wander over to the inn,	e
Oasis for the chip-starved inner bard,	f
Ecstatic overload assured where gin,	e
Tobacco, gossip mingle in the yard.	f
Renewed, refreshed, the poets generate	g
Yeast for the spirit, and they celebrate.	g

You can adapt acrostics by adjusting the form in various different ways. You can reverse the pattern by using the last letter of each line instead of the first to spell out a word (a telestich). You could create a whole sentence by using the opening word of each line, rather than just its first letter, or again use the final word of the line.

The only snag is that the device can slip by unnoticed. Some poets print acrostics with bold type for the appropriate letters, or extra spacing. Others leave all the text the same, allowing readers to stumble on the acrostic by happy chance, but knowing that not all will find it.

Rime Royal

This seven line stanza is a good vehicle for lyric, narrative and descriptive poems. It's the form used by Chaucer in his *Troilus and Criseyde*, and it was also used by Shakespeare. It is usually written in iambic pentameter, and rhymes: a b a b b c c.

Stanzas from EYAM
(a poem about Derbyshire's plague village)

The tailor sent to London for a bolt	a
of finest cloth for dressing gentlemen,	b
not dreaming that the worsted for a coat	a
would be the stuff that spread contagion when	b
he measured lengths for cutting it. But then	b
he did not know his cloth was full of fleas	c
that carried traces of a vile disease.	c
Plague showed itself in fever, coughs and sores.	d
The tailor and his landlady were first	e
to suffer, and as one by one, then scores	d
of friends and neighbours yielded, they grew worse.	/e
No family was spared. The village, cursed,	e
saw daily sacrifice; fears multiplied	f
as fathers, mothers, children sickened, died.	f

Exercises

26. Think of a place you would like to immortalise in poetry, and something you could add to the snapshot description to give the poem an extra dimension. Craft a poem in saphhic quatrains or as an acrostic.

27. Write your own persona poem in blank verse, looking at a well known story – fairy tales, familiar plays and novels, biblical or historical stories are ideal – and describing and/or commenting on the events in the voice of one of the characters involved. (There's a fairy tale example at the end of chapter 7.)

28. Compile a cento on any theme, remembering to use work that is out of copyright, and to attribute each source. Include some lines of your own if you wish.

29. Make up a riddle, either using letter clues as in the example given here, or a punning conundrum in the style of the traditional: *When is a door not a door? When it's ajar.* Remember, though, that in this case we are looking for a brief poem, and not just a one-liner.

30. Think up a situation in which circumstances turn an event from something good to something bad – or vice versa. Write a dizain, with the change of circumstances occurring in the middle of the poem.

31. Write up an observation that has made a lasting impression on you, using either Burns stanzas or rime royal.

Answer to the riddle: earth.

Chapter 6

Numbers and Pictures

All the forms we have looked at so far depend on the application of patterns in the rhyme and/or metre of the poem. There are many other forms that have no rhyming or metrical requirement, because a count of syllables or a shape on the page is the defining factor that identifies poetry.

Many of the forms are very short, and unless particular content is specified, they tend to be most useful for poetic fragments, brief descriptions, little cameos of observation or imagination.

Syllabic poems exist in various languages and cultures; and therein lies a problem. Not all languages can be translated with exact parallels, and precision is required where something as finely balanced as a count of syllables is concerned. In fact, within an individual language there can be some confusion. We've already considered, in the example of a rondel, how elision can shorten a word, and how a long vowel sound may be pronounced as one or two syllables. Couple this possible complication with the intricacy of another language and its translation, and you can see that syllable counts are not as cut-and-dried as they might seem.

Syllabics that originated in Japan are particularly tricky, and when editors are asking for the first of these forms we're considering, they may specify '5-7-5.'

Haiku

The most popular Japanese form is extremely short, and yet has to embrace various points. A haiku is a delicate poem of three lines, which has been described as 'a moment of intense perception.' It's one of those forms to which the cliché applies, that it takes a moment to learn and a lifetime to master. It is made up of three lines, with five syllables on the first line, seven on the second and five on the third.

As we have just seen, this syllable count is open to interpretation, and it is not unusual to see any tiny fragment, usually but not invariably with three lines, referred to as a haiku. Obviously, the haiku's message must be communicated in a very taut, condensed form. The poem is not merely a collection of syllables. It should be compatible with Zen philosophy, and there should be references in its words to the natural world, and to seasons and time. These references may be overt, or discreetly masked. The words *tree in winter* show plainly what *frosted leaves* imply.

The form is subdivided into two categories: the actual haiku, which looks into the nature of the universe, and the senryu, which focuses on the nature of man. Two added nuances of its construction are that there should be a subtle turn after the second line, providing a fine shift in the poem; and that the content of the piece should be open ended, suggesting that there may be more to come.

Traditionally there is no title, but the form's name is given in its place. The first example is a haiku, the second a senryu.

HAIKU

Midsummer sun spills
molten gold that catches breath;
fills the sea with fire.

HAIKU

Shortest day over,
Christmas offers warmth and friends,
fills us with promise.

Tanka

At almost double the length of the haiku, its older parent form has two extra lines of seven syllables each, to produce a syllable count of 5 7 5 7 7, although these figures are again subject to discussion because of the comparative natures of the Japanese and English languages. In this form, the turn occurs after the third line.

TANKA

I count reflections,
infinity of mirrors -
boneless likenesses.
I wonder where thought shrivels,
diminished emotions end.

Cinquains

A much more recent form of syllabic poetry was devised in America by Adelaide Crapsey at the start of the twentieth century. It has twenty-two syllables arranged on five lines in the pattern: 2 4 6 8 2. Like the Japanese forms, it has no rhyming or metrical requirement.

SCALE

Orange
and gold stripes prowl
the garden; ginger cat
in wet grass mimics rainforest
tigers.

The cinquain can be used as a stanza pattern, with any number of cinquains contributing to the poem.

Rhymed Syllabics

There are some forms of syllabic poetry which also make use of rhyme, and probably the most popular of these are the Welsh forms. They can be used as a complete poem, often untitled, or as the stanzas in a longer work.

Englyns or Englynion

These are very early forms in the Welsh poetry tradition. There are eight different types of englyn, six of which are quatrains. We'll look at two popular styles.

The englyn unodl union has thirty syllables in four lines with a count of: 10 6 6 7. Although there is no rhyme at the end of the first line, its 6th, 7th, 8th or 9th syllable rhymes with the other three lines, to form: a:x a a a

PTAH

Forever seated in shade, the great god   a:x

of darkness is portrayed   a
in stone, with shadows splayed   a
to mask him where men invade.   a

An englyn cyrch also has four lines, but these are of seven syllables each. The first, second and fourth lines rhyme together, while the third line rhymes with one of the three middle syllables in the fourth, giving a pattern of: a a b b:a

OAK

Ancient oak branches spread wide,   a

drop acorns to seed beside   a
the parent tree; anchor, shoot   b

where legend and root collide.   b:a

Clogyrnach

This is only a slightly longer form than the englyn, with six lines taking the syllable pattern: 8 8 5 5 3 3. Sometimes the last two lines are combined, giving: 8 8 5 5 6. There are two rhymes in the poem, so that the six-line version rhymes: a a b b b a, and the five-liner: a a b b b:a.

SKETCH

A few strokes bring to life a day   a

destined to be remembered; splay   a
of light on sea, shells   b
and pebbles, sand, wells   b
of joy, swells   b
where waves play.   a
OR
of joy, swells where waves play.   b/a

Four Square

Devised in the twenty-first century, this is a simple form, but fascinating. Like the patterns we have just looked at, it relies on a count, but in this case the words themselves are counted, regardless of the number of syllables. It is made up of four stanzas, each of which has four lines, each of which has four words, so the complete poem is only sixty-four words long.

There is no rhyming or metrical requirement, but a four square should have a title. It is a form that suggests balance, and each stanza should look at the poem's theme in a slightly different way. It could be four sides of an argument, or a nostalgic piece with four fragments of memory, or a situation shown through the eyes of four different people. As each viewpoint needs to be expressed in sixteen words, economy of language is paramount.

This example shows a simple list, but you will note that every stanza has a shifted emphasis.

CLUTTER

Her bedroom is chaos
of lipsticks, discarded dresses,
washing mountains, unpaired shoes,
an avalanche of handbags.   (grown-up factors)

Here are mugs growing
new strains of bacteria;
chocolate wrappers, crisp packets
and half a sandwich.   (teen nutrition factors)

A teddy bear guards
mobile and tablet; part
completed, an almost jigsaw
sulks among felt tips.   (childhood remnants)

Disorder rules. Her room
is a tantrum where
school books and mascara
show child, show woman.   (status summary)

Spatial Poetry

Having looked at the numbers, it's time to think about the pictures. Readers are accustomed to the general shape of a poem on the page, and can tell at a glance whether a piece of writing is poetry or prose – bringing to mind the child's definition of poetry as 'writing that doesn't reach the edge.' As soon as poetry became a written rather than an oral craft, its appearance became significant. As far back as around 300 BC the Greeks began using shaped patterns for poems. George Herbert's *Easter Wings*, published in 1633, is a frequently quoted example of the form, and since the mid twentieth century there has been an explosion of spatial poetry.

Concrete poems are ideogrammic images, where the message of the poem is reinforced by a picture made from the letters and words of its structure. While it is good if the poem works when it is read aloud, its message really only comes through when seen on the page.

HIDE AND SEEK

1 2 3 4 5
6 7 8 9 10
11 12 13 14 15 ...
Coming, ready or not!

seek   seek seek   h

seek *cold*   seek *warmer*   *HOT*   i

cold   seek   *warmer*   d

GOTCHA!   e

Positive calligrammes are formed when a body of text takes a specific shape, relevant to the subject, within which the poem is printed, as shown in the example. In a negative calligramme, the words would appear around white space, again in an appropriate shape.

BECALMED

I

try

to catch

the wind, fill

my sails with warm
blown breezes; but they
stay resolutely limp, becalmed,
leaving me adrift, frustrated, stilled.

And I realise that I should be enjoying full sun, lying on the deck,
feeling
heat prickle my skin while I eat mango and coconut, while I
drink rum
punch from a long, long glass. And still I yearn for air and
motion.

It is easy to see that the poet is indebted to developments in word processing for the ability to centre text at the press of a button. Any symmetrical shape is ridiculously easy to forge. If you like to write seasonal poetry, a Christmas tree or an Easter egg is a must. You can, of course, create more complex shapes; but symmetrical ones are the easiest to start with and build your confidence.

Exercises

32. Experiment with the haiku, looking for the moment of perception that will bring it to life, and the nature/season references.

33. Using the same theme as for the haiku, write the more extended tanka, observing a turn after the third line. Look at the two poems. Which works better, and why?

34. Devise a cinquain describing a landscape or urban scene. Using it as an opening stanza, develop a longer poem introducing some narrative, but retaining the cinquain pattern for each stanza.

35. Make a list of themes that could be covered within the confines of an englyn or clogyrnach. Select one to try in a range of short syllabic forms. Which form is most effective, and which the most enjoyable to produce?

36. Try out some ideas for positive and negative calligrammes. Do they work when spoken aloud, or is the pattern on the page the only route to appreciation of the poem?

37. Experiment with the four square, thinking up some subjects that have the potential to be considered from four angles, then trying them out to see which is the most effective.

Chapter 7

Free Verse – Or Is It?

In a book about forms, you may be wondering about the inclusion of free verse, which by definition sounds like the anti-form. In fact it's nothing of the kind, and assuming the content of the poem works, its success relies on careful application of technique. While in set forms this means length, rhyme and metre, in free verse the ingredients are a little more subtle.

Free verse is not the easy option. It involves rather more planning than any of the strict forms. When you have selected the best set form for your poem, you have a well-defined pattern of rules to follow. Get them right, and your writing is well on the way to becoming an accomplished poem. Careful checking of the poem's length, rhyme scheme, line length and application of metre will show if you are getting them wrong, and you will know at once what it is you need to address.

There is also a question mark over your writing's identity as an actual poem. If there are full rhyme and metre, even if they display inaccuracies, readers will recognise a poem. If there are not, you have to convince them by your use of language and skill in crafting that this is definitely not a piece of prose. Your poem will stand or fall by how convincing you are.

Writing a set form poem involves pouring your ideas into a mould and working out whether they fit. If they don't, you can always find a different mould. In free verse, you are working freehand, constructing the shape even as you put the words and lines together. Few poets set out to write a free verse poem with a fixed idea about line and stanza length. Patterns may emerge when words start to hit paper, and they can begin to create a mould for the poem; but the important thing to remember is that at the start you are having to build from nothing.

To use a domestic image, it's rather like making a garment. You can cut out pieces of material according to a pattern and stitch them together, or you can take wool and needles, cast on, and build your work into a shape as you develop it. The course you follow is determined by the nature of garment you are producing. Wool will tell you it needs to be a jumper, material a shirt. The subject of your poem will tell you whether it needs a set form or a free verse treatment. Get it wrong and no amount of alteration and teasing will put it right; you will have to unravel it and start again.

The decision to use free verse means you actively need to avoid certain devices of set forms. Your poem will be weakened if you launch into full rhyme or iambic pentameter half way through, and even more so if you later abandon these elements. There is a rider. Your poem will be weakened by doing this unless there is a sound artistic reason for it. For example, the subject of a wild horse running free that is broken and tamed could easily justify a form that begins in free verse and gravitates towards the 'straitjacket' of rhyme and metre.

While avoiding the factors that make up set forms, you need to be aware of the three dominant elements of free verse, which are use of language, slant rhyme and shape.

Good use of language means that vocabulary is well selected, so that it would be impossible to imagine any other word at that point in the poem. The words can be plain and straightforward, without any need for over-flowery, aggressively poetical vocabulary. It pays to think about any nuances of baggage they carry with them, in order to avoid or capitalise on a resonance for the reader.

Figurative language communicates your message to best advantage. Make use of similes and the stronger metaphors. Include images to appeal to the senses, which makes the writing more memorable for the reader.

Be aware of the sounds produced by your chosen words. This

means both taking advantage of onomatopoeia to create an effect, using words whose sound resembles their meaning, like *buzz* and *hiss*; and considering whether the consonants in your words are plosive or sustained, the vowels short monophthongs or longer diphthongs, to give your writing a 'feel' of briskness or lethargy, wakefulness or tiredness, openness or insidiousness.

Guard against lazy wording. You can usually strengthen a poem by removing a bland verb qualified by an adverb, and substituting a stronger verb. Careful selection of adjectives means that you can convey as much in one that is absolutely right as in three that come close. Overuse of even the smallest words can grate. (*The* is a serial offender.)

While full rhyme is not wanted, slant rhyme is a major part of a free verse poem. Any similarity of sound that stops short of the full rhyme's chiming *moon/June* effect can be used as slant rhyme. So we are looking for examples of:

- assonance. Vowel sounds match but the consonants at the end of them do not, eg. *cool food*.
- alliteration, where the same consonant sound is used to begin consecutive or nearby words, eg. *babbling brook*.
- consonance, where the same consonant sound is used to end consecutive or nearby words, eg. *great height*.
- full consonance, in which words begin and end with the same sounds, eg. *wild wood*.
- unaccented rhyme, with final unstressed syllables rhyming although previous syllables that bear the stress do not, eg. *arriving walking*.
- eye rhyme, where the appearance of the word looks as if the sound will be the same, but its pronunciation is not, eg. *cover over*.
- synthetic rhyme wrenches the pronunciation to produce a rhyme, eg. Hilaire Belloc's brilliant matching of *later* and *theatre* – pronounced *thee-ay-ter*.

- crossed syllable rhyme produces full rhyme between syllables in different positions in the words, eg. *regret* with *setting* or *letterhead*.
- half rhyme matches the final stressed syllable of a word, but there are different unstressed syllables following, eg. *slavish* and *caving*.

The terms are included for interest. A working poet needs to have a sensitivity to sound similarities rather than the ability to know the difference between assonance and consonance. In general, if any sound in one word matches any sound in another, slant rhyme is coming into play.

A single example of slant rhyme has little impact, and could be a mere quirk of pronunciation; but repeated use of them instils a sense of poetry and provides a subtle network of sound effects that holds the piece together as a poem. While the line's end seems the obvious place to deploy slant rhymes, they can also be scattered throughout the lines to create an even more pleasing effect.

There is nothing arbitrary about the way a free verse poem is shaped. Its presentation is part of its ability to communicate a message with clarity. If it is set out correctly, it is easy to read, and the reader wastes no time trying to work out how to phrase the sentences. If the layout is not helpful, the reader's concentration is drawn away from the content of the poem and focussed on deciding where one phrase ends and the next begins.

At the start of the writing, you need to decide whether or not to break the text into stanzas. Presentation as a solid chunk works well for concentrated ideas in poems that are not too long. Stanza breaks make it easier to digest the poem, particularly if it is twenty lines or more in length. There is no mystique about knowing when to start a new stanza. It occurs when there's a new impulse of material, just as a fresh paragraph works in a prose passage. Sometimes it's appropriate to work all your stanzas into the same number of lines each, but there's nothing wrong with having stanzas of widely differing lengths.

Remember that if you start a pattern, there needs to be a good reason for failing to sustain it. So if you begin your free verse poem with six quatrain stanzas, don't suddenly change to three lines in the next and eight in the next. Or of you start with varied lengths, don't gravitate to all five-line stanzas towards the end.

Line breaks are trickier, and of course these need to be addressed whether you are using separate stanzas or a single block of text. There are two points to consider. First, remember that there is always a hint of extra emphasis on the last word of a line of poetry. The eye lingers there for a tiny fraction of a second before moving into the next line. A speaker will take an infinitesimal pause to indicate an enjambment, so even if there is no punctuation, a hint of extra weight colours that final word. A significant word should be placed there to take advantage of that minuscule pause, benefiting from the extra emphasis it provides. It's a pity to squander such a delicate stress by allowing it to rest on a weak or 'worker' word such as *the* or *in*.

The other point relies on the phrasing. If a line break severs a phrase at an illogical place, it reads awkwardly. This doesn't mean every line has to be endstopped; we've already considered the use of enjambment. But it does suggest that using the line breaks to separate one phrase from another is an additional way of ensuring an easy read for anyone studying your work.

Cultivate the habit of listening to the tempo of each individual line to ensure its dynamics are working. Listen in your head first, then read your work aloud to confirm your observations.

Let's have a look at two free verse poems, using different techniques. The first started life as a single block of text, but was divided into two stanzas where there was a shift of approach from biological fact to personal action.

57%

More than half of me is water
trapped in bone and muscle,
pumped through arteries, turned to saliva,
bile and sweat. This water knows
no trilling over stream-bed's pebbles
seeking rivers, dancing out to sea;
no pull of breeze to vaporise in clouds,
free fall and drench parched gardens.
Instead it keeps my skin from desiccating,
brain from atrophying, heart and liver
from being ground to dust.

I open a bottle. Uncapped, it bubbles over.
I feel water fizz on my tongue,
sense its elation to escape
constraint of glass. It slips down my gullet,
settles, complacent, in my stomach -
does not know consummation will make it
my better half.

Many of the lines are end-stopped, but where there is an enjambment, the last word of the line is a strong one; or at least that is the case until we reach the penultimate line. *It* could hardly be described as a strong word, but its placing is phrase-based so that the sense of the phrase is not awkwardly severed. The last line, echoing the first, wants to stand alone.

The use of language includes plays on words, such as *ground* which describes the act of grinding but echoes the idea of the earth, the resonance of *to dust* with the wording of the funeral service, and that of the last line with the expression for a loved partner. The device of personification allows the water to be *complacent* and to sense *elation*.

Slant rhymes have been used at line ends with the neutral vowel sound creating unaccented rhyme in *water/saliva/liver/over*. There is internal slant rhyming in close proximity, a few examples being the alliteration of *free fall*, assonance of *bed's pebbles, parched gardens*, unaccented rhyme in *seeking* and *dancing*, consonance in *breeze* and *vaporise*, and full consonance with *slips* and *settles*.

While the first poem was built around observation and comment, this next one is a narrative persona poem, where Red Riding Hood's wolf has his say, the fantasy aspect being underlined by the sheer impossibility of recounting the tale after the events of the first two lines.

NOT MY FAULT

It isn't quick, it isn't painless
when someone hacks your head off,
chopping through flesh and fat,
bone and sinew with an axe. You feel
each blow resonating in your limbs,
know blood's spurt in your fur.

And I am not to blame; it is my nature
to eat when food appears, use wiles
to get my way. If anyone's at fault
it's a mother who lets her idiot child
skip through my forest in blaring red,
her basket stuffed with pies and cake.

I approached her, asked her first,
and she refused to share. So who's surprised
I ran ahead and hid and waited?
The nightgown? That was a masterstroke,
although in truth I didn't really look

like Granny. Her mistake
shows once again the girl's stupidity.

I'd have been happy with a piece of pie
but hunger overtook, and she looked
so succulent with those plump little arms,
delicious round belly.

She started that inane conversation -
big ears, big eyes, big teeth. Did no-one tell her
how rude it is to make personal remarks?

My mouth was watering by then.
I knew how tasty she'd be,
could not stop my jaws from slavering.
Then there he stood, axe menacing,
eyes filled with hate. And here I am,

feeling pain subside at last
as rigor sets in, and the forest's scavengers
are moving closer to peck my eyes,
worm through my coat, leave maggot eggs
to fatten on dead flesh. It's not my fault.
It's not.
Not.

This illustrates the way poems begin new stanzas where prose
would start a new paragraph. An apparent break in the pattern
occurs between the last two stanzas. It might be more logical to
end the penultimate stanza at the full stop, and start the next
with *And here I am*, but the device of moving into a new stanza
part way through the sentence is designed to suggest the wolf's
disorientation – understandable after decapitation.

Here, too, breaks are designed to leave a strong word at the line end. The question of line dynamics arises at the close of the poem. Up to that point, the lines are all of similar length. The odd disjointed words on the shortest ones indicate the wolf's fading.

The tone is conversational for the narration of the story, while employing economy of language by using words to imply more than they say, such as *worm through my coat*, or *axe menacing*. The language also demonstrates the value of repetition, with *big*'s repeats to chime with the fairytale and build up tension, and *it's not* at the end for emphasis.

Slant rhyme features in the alliteration of *hacks your head* or *flesh and fat*, assonance of *spurt* and *fur*, or *wiles* with *child* and *pies*. There is consonance in *ahead and hid and waited*, and full consonance in *masterstroke* and *mistake*, unaccented rhyme in *stupidity* and *happy*, in *watering, slavering* and *menacing*, and eye rhyme in *blood* and *food*.

Although all of the elements we have looked at contribute – hopefully – to the effectiveness of the poem, fretting about them during the writing process can inhibit your flow of thought and weaken the overall effect. Often slant rhyme can be introduced during the revision process, when within the richness of language we can spot an alternative word to introduce similarity of sound, and make a substitution.

Exercises

38. Select any word of one syllable. Write down a few of its full rhymes, then concentrate on the slant rhymes, using as many styles of slant rhyme as you can. See if your word lists have threads of ideas beginning that could belong within the same poem.

39. Take a free verse poem written by another poet, and look carefully at every line. Can you find any points where

different words could have been substituted to bring in more examples of slant rhyme?

40. Begin with any of your own poems of at least eight lines written in a set form, and try to re-work it as a free verse poem. You may use exactly the same content, or you may need to adjust it. Which is better? Why?

41. Create a free verse poem looking at both the technical and human side of any scientific fact, from a vast subject like gravity or electricity, to a consideration of how long it takes your fingernails to grow. Explore the information beginning with a single block of text, and then decide whether and where to include stanza breaks.

42. Collect together half a dozen free verse poems written by anyone other than yourself. Read them all aloud, asking yourself whether their use of language sounds more like poetry or prose. This exercise helps to refine your answer to the regularly offered criticism of free verse as 'just prose chopped up and put on different lines.'

43. Write a free verse poem about something you have seen in a museum or a stately home. There may be elements of description, analysis, historical fact, nostalgia and imaginative input. Try to avoid writing something which gives the reader nothing but a snapshot view of the item, which is rarely a memorable device.

Chapter 8

Where to Next?

The history of prosody is littered with examples of set forms moving through time, space and cultures, and being adapted and adjusted in the process. Those of us who write poetry today inherit the legacy of all the poets who went before, and move the craft on for the benefit of the next generations of poets.

When you feel completely comfortable with a range of set forms, there's something incredibly satisfying about tweaking them to add your own variants. Sonnets, for example, with their long history, have undergone many changes, and today's writers continue to adapt them. There have been unrhymed sonnets, new rhyme schemes, and even tinkering with the fourteen line length. Some have been successful, others not so; but the joy of experimentation is the knowledge that the result may fall flat, or it may change the world.

A desire to adjust a standard form should arise from a wish to make a better vehicle for a poem, not just because you think it would be mathematically interesting to play with the lines or syllables. You may wish to try a new version of a form for a single poem you want to write, because the shape you are planning seems so much better than the original. If an adaptation works for one subject, it could work for others. If it has general appeal, you are on the way to moving the form forwards.

You may prefer to start from scratch, and devise an entirely new form. This involves making a lot more decisions than the adjustment of an established form requires. You will need to consider how many lines the form will have, and whether it will be a stanza pattern or a complete poem in itself. You will need to choose whether to have a single line length throughout, varied lengths, or a regular pattern of different lengths.

The metrical feet will need some thought. Different patterns elicit different emotional responses from readers. Iambic metre, with its insistent *di-dum, di-dum* beat reflects the sound of the human heart – the first sound we know even before we are born. So it has a comfort factor which can have the most subtle influence on the reader. A galloping rhythm, full of anapaests, impresses urgency. A form with a lot of spondees implies gravity, and so on.

Your choice of full or slant rhyme will also influence readers. Full rhyme has a satisfying, safe feel to it – even if your poem is on a disturbing subject. Slant rhymes are more edgy. Repetition can lull or insist.

There may be an opportunity to link different ideas for your form together, such as having interleaved stanzas, with one set of stanzas in free verse and the alternate ones in strictly rhymed quatrains. Repetition may be included, a syllable count, or a quirk of presentation.

Don't forget to name your form. It's far better to call it something by which it will be recognised than to have it known for ever as *oh yes, one of those daft new poems*.

Up to now, the subject matter in your adjusted or newly devised form has hardly been mentioned. If this can develop alongside your form, well and good; but there's one important warning to take on board whenever you are inventing forms, just as when you are using a traditional pattern. Always remember that the poem's content is the vital material. The form is its servant, not its master.

It's absorbing and exciting to develop set forms and invent new ones. An even more interesting project is to create a longer poem that uses a range of different forms. This first person biographical example shows how a shift from one area of subject matter to the next can be pointed by the insertion of a different form instead of simply using stanza breaks. All the forms included are unrhymed, but of course rhyme could have been used.

DREDGING DIAMONDS

I remember sitting under the table,
leaves collapsed to form a rigid cat's-cradle around me
smelling of wood and lavender wax,
of dinners and teas, don't talk with your mouth full,
elbows off. Andy Pandy, Looby Loo and Teddy
have the hamper's wicker lid closed on their heads.
I cry. Mum makes her only complaint to the BBC.

I'm holding Mummy's hand in big school,
and Jill's there holding her Mummy's hand,
and we're big girls now so we don't cry.
Just two weeks later we move house,
and I have to find a way to fill new spaces
in rooms that echo the wrong sounds,
in a classroom where everyone else has a best friend.

(free verse)

A tiny pink girl
snuffles and snuggles, makes us
a whole family.   (haiku - senryu)

Beyond the Biggest Spotty Dog in the World
I find the oldest music teacher in the world,
learn scales and songs until Beethoven rolls over
to make room for the Beatles, Monkees, the Beach Boys;
and boys.   (free verse)

We move
again, and I,
wrenched from school, youth club, friends,
become the teenaged monster, vile
wild child.   (cinquain)

Dad conjures a respite,
rings the local theatre, introduces me;
I pause mid-protest to audition.
I'm watching as the set collapses,
exposes shamefaced stagehands; look at one
   and
Romeo and Juliet
   Antony and Cleopatra
      Albert and Victoria
         Tristan and Isolde
            Napoleon and Josephine
are downgraded to passing fancies.
This is Love.   (free verse including spatial element)

The sky never looked
like this before, gunmetal
grey, hot, holding time
while the *I do* promises
ricochet around the stars.   (tanka)

I am spattered head to foot with peach emulsion.
Our three year old daughter stays with Nana and Grandad
when I rush to the hospital.
Her baby sister arrives - prompt, quick, tidy, efficient -
setting the future pattern.

There follows a chaos of trips to the park,
treks through Pompei, batches of scones baked and shared,
Sunday roasts and a game of cards, choosing a kitten,
feeding squirrels, letters to Santa, swimming the pool's
   length.
Passing parcels and musical chairs
count years and minutes, merge and bed themselves deep
in the morass of time as it spirals ever faster.   (free verse)

But no weight
of ordinary days
dims the diamonds.   (word count 3x3)

To offer an oxymoron, this is a very short long poem. A much longer piece demonstrating the form change technique would be something like Alice Oswald's wonderful *Dart*, about the river. But even a short long poem can offer you the scope to play with forms and let them intermingle. This allows you to control the tempo of the poem, where the texture of different forms can speed or slow the work for the reader.

Because of the composite nature of this poem, a point about balance can be introduced. We begin with a lot of details about the subject's early years. We travel twenty-two lines, a third of the poem, before we reach the onset of adolescence. By contrast, the final free verse stanza crams about twenty years into seven lines. The intention is to show how time crawls when you're young, but gallops when you're an adult, eased by the division into sections. The spatial area of the poem is designed to show that heart-stopping moment when the world changes, so the pattern will – hopefully – draw the reader's eye through the content at speed, but hint at the world-shattering events taking place.

It may be that the idea of adapting or coming up with new forms holds no interest for you, but you still like the challenge of trying new forms. They are emerging all the time, and the writers who devise them are delighted to have other people taking them up. Needless to say, not all of them work, and many fizzle out almost as soon as they're planned; but you can find plenty of information about them, most of it from the internet.

Poets love to blog about new patterns they've thought up, and poetry workshop websites are always featuring novel forms. Some suggest appropriate subject matter, others leave it to the writers.

The range of small press poetry magazines rarely features

new forms, but it has been known. A good poetry club, class or circle should be a source of information about them. Magazines about the craft of writing may include such information as well.

All these outlets will introduce you to new forms to try; and of course they are available for you to showcase the information you want to share when you have created a form and want it to be better known.

In addition to these, you can introduce a new form at an open mic event if you're brave enough, allowing the audience to be the first people to experience it. Could you interest a creative writing tutor in it, and ask for it to be used as an exercise in classes? If you give talks and workshops, you have a captive audience to enthral.

You could even launch a competition for poems in your form, either on a small local basis or by branching out into the wider world of writers. It's a good way to get more and more people using it, who then feed it into their own networks so that information about it spreads exponentially. Remember to publish relevant instructions about the form and any restrictions on content alongside the rules of your competition, together with a technically perfect example if you wish to offer this additional help.

If you decide to follow this route, it's useful to pair up with someone – or some organisation – with experience of running poetry competitions, in order to work out funding, adjudication procedures, prizes, publicity and the best rules to include. But what may sound like a daunting task is just another amazing foray into the poetry world.

The whole business of writing poetry is an adventure. By exploring all the different set forms, from rhyming couplets to free verse, and inventing your own, the adventure takes on new dimensions and new excitements.

Exercises

44. This book lists over fifty different forms and variants. Scour your poetry collections and the internet to find some that are not mentioned here, and experiment with them.

45. Take a tightly rhymed short form, such as a triolet or Chaucerian roundel, and adapt it by adding another three or four lines, introducing a third rhyming sound. Work out how you will space the extra lines, and follow the same metrical pattern as the rest of the poem. Now find a piece by another poet in the original form, and try expanding it in your new direction, purely as an exercise. The next part of the exercise is to perform the same task on one of your own poems in the original form. The final stage is to create a complete new poem in this virgin form, incorporating three rhyming sounds.

46. Start with a small nugget of information or a cameo of description you would like to incorporate into a poem. Make sure it's a tiny, limited subject and not a vast concept. Now devise a syllable count or word count form to accommodate it. When you have worked the example, leave it for a day or two, and then create another poem in the same syllable or word count on a different subject.

47. Take any free verse poem you have written, and change its tone by adding a refrain at regular intervals, such as at the start or the end of each stanza. Does this enhance or spoil the poem? How and why?

48. Put together an autobiographical poem of between forty and eighty lines, using passages of free verse interspersed with different forms. This doesn't have to be a 'whole life'

autobiography – you may choose to write about half a dozen anecdotes that occurred during your first term at senior school, for example, or bring together events, emotions and reactions connected with a special holiday, with falling in love, with a bereavement, with a house move.

49. Devise a schedule for popularising your newly-invented form, perhaps including some of the ideas suggested, and also adding your own.

50. Go through the poems you have written and practise reading them aloud. This exercise has two functions. First, you will gain confidence in the readings, especially if you concentrate on projecting your voice as if to fill a hall; then giving a reading of your work will not be such a daunting task. You will also have the opportunity to spot any awkwardness of rhythm or flow, or any lines which are clumsily constructed. If you hesitate on a line once, it's a slip of the tongue. Hesitate at the same point again, and it may be some flaw in the writing that needs attention.

Finally, whenever you have a few minutes to spare, remember that reading poetry is the best possible activity for poets. Look at set form poetry to see how other poets have handled it through the years, but concentrate particularly on contemporary writing as an inspiration for your own work.

Having spent some time on set forms, look at a range of free verse poems, again concentrating on the most recent work you can find.

Check out your reactions to both by asking yourself if you like a particular poem, whether it conveys its message with clarity, whether the form selected was the best vehicle for communicating that subject matter, and what makes it successful. See if you can work out why the poet decided on that particular format for expressing ideas.

Your observations on these readings will inform your own writing far into the future, and demonstrate new patterns for you to explore. Enjoy the reading, and you will enjoy your writing all the more.

COMPASS
BOOKS

Compass Books focuses on practical and informative 'how-to' books for writers. Written by experienced authors who also have extensive experience of tutoring at the most popular creative writing workshops, the books offer an insight into the more specialised niches of the publishing game.